IDAHO

SNAKE RIVER

SAWTOOTH RANGE

Pendleton

BLUE MOUNTAINS

rch
k Battle

Granite

on City

Ironside

Malheur Agency

np Harney

Stone
House

Boise

Malheur Lake

OWYHEE RIVER

MIS

SNAKE RIVER

Fort Lyon

Sheep
Ranch

Silver City

Jordan Cr.

Open
Valley

Rattlesnake Cr.

Camp Three Forks

Fort Hall

Antelope Cr.

Duck

Valley

Fort McDermit

HUMBOLDT RIVER

Winnemucca

Elko

NEVADA

Sarah Winnemucca

Sarah Winnemucca

Most Extraordinary Woman of the Paiute Nation

by Katherine Gehm

Published by
O'SULLIVAN
WOODSIDE
& COMPANY
Phoenix, Arizona

Manufactured in the United States of America

Published by

**O'SULLIVAN
WOODSIDE
& COMPANY**

2218 East Magnolia
Phoenix, Arizona 85034

Library of Congress Cataloging in Publication Data

Gehm, Katherine.
    Sarah Winnemucca: most extraordinary woman of
the Paiute nation.

    Bibliography: p.
    SUMMARY: A biography of an Indian princess who
spent her life working for better treatment for her
people by the United States government.
    1. Hopkins, Sarah Winnemucca, 1844?-1891.
2. Paiute Indians. [1. Hopkins, Sarah Winnemucca,
1844?-1891. 2. Paiute Indians--Biography. 3. Indians of North America--Biography] I. Title.
E99.P2H698   973'.04'97 [B] [92]   75-12600
ISBN 0-89019-030-5

To Jake, John and Jory

Foreword

Sarah Winnemucca was a privileged woman. As the daughter of the Paiutes' Chief, Winnemucca II, certain doors were open to her which would not have been available to one who was not a princess. But as one reads the story of Sarah, he realizes those doors had little to do with her achievements. Far more important was the fact that she was an intelligent woman who, through those doors, found education and then confidence in herself, and used her abilities for the benefit of her people.

A person of achievement is often criticized as having used individuals for personal gain. Sarah was not denied such criticism. She had a talent for language and with that gift she was able first to work as a translator and later to speak out against the Indian Agents who used the Indians for their own gain. The well-organized efforts to defame her hurt Sarah personally, but she continued her verbal attacks on those whites who prospered by using what belonged to the Indian for their own advancement.

Over the years Sarah's grandfather and her father pleaded the cause of peace with the white man. Throughout her life she shared this family feeling even though at every turn of events it seemed that the cause was not just and filled only with promises that were never meant to be kept.

Sarah Winnemucca was a privileged woman in the most beautiful sense. When her beauty and intelligence could have taken her from the reservation into a sophisticated city life, she remained with her people to fight for them. During the Bannock War she attempted to persuade the Indians to stop the bloodshed and in so doing risked her own life. In her short life the education of the Indian was another concern.

The author of this exciting story of Sarah Winnemucca gives the reader insight into an Indian woman whose place in America's history has been neglected too long.

Harold H.J. Erickson

Director of Libraries
University of Nevada, Las Vegas

Preface

During my years of research on Indians of the West, I became fascinated with the life of Sarah Winnemucca and believe her to be one of the classic red women of all time.

In the 1880s, Sarah's stormy crusade for Indian justice reached across the nation. Because she had the courage to publicize facts of corruption within the Indian Bureau, through lectures to the American people, she became the target for a great deal of personal abuse. However, charges made against her character were met and refuted by many friends.

A specific purpose in writing this story is to provide the reader with information concerning the Indian princess and to characterize her as a woman. A secondary purpose is to stress her dedication to the interests and welfare of Nevada Paiutes and to acquaint the reader with Sarah Winnemucca's aid to the United States through her constant efforts to bring about peace and understanding between her race and the white one.

Material is presented from the Indians' point of view and written for general reader interest. Differences of opinion concerning Sarah's dedicated life and an inconsistency of historical records were frequently found. In such cases, I accepted the most reliable source and followed through to logical conclusions. With the exception of direct quotes from Sarah's book *Life Among the Piutes—Their Wrongs and Claims* (1883), thoughts and words of the various characters are given as I have interpreted them through extensive research. A sincere effort has been made on my part to bring Sarah alive through dialogue and dramatization of historical events while still holding to the essential truth.

From the bottom of my heart I wish to thank each and every person who gave me help and encouragement in making the publication of this book possible.

Sarah Winnemucca

» 1

A casual visitor to Secretary of the Interior Carl Schurz's office on one cold and snowy January morning in 1880 would have been in for a surprise as he entered the formal reception room. Sitting quietly on uncomfortable, straight-backed chairs were three Indians of Nevada's Paiute tribe, two men and a woman, patiently waiting to "make words" with the secretary.

They formed a striking picture. The woman of perhaps thirty-five years was stunning in a native Paiute dress of natural colored deerskin. Rows of beaded fringe trimmed her skirt's lower edge and again at the waist. An elaborate yoke encircled a high neckline. An oval face radiated charm, courage and intelligence with evidence of determination touching the corners of her well-shaped mouth. The man on her right was much older, his face lined and weathered, his eyes deceptively gentle at the moment. The one on her left was a handsome young brave whose bronze skin was clear and smooth, and whose lustrous black hair hung straight, reaching almost to his shoulders.

The two men wore ill-fitting army uniforms which should have detracted from their dignity, had it been possible. But this was Winnemucca II, Big Chief of Nevada Paiutes, and his son Natchez, a sub-chief. The proud lift of their heads and their regal carriage rose above any humiliation white men might heap upon them. The woman was Sarah, daughter of the chieftain. All three had come East following an invitation from President Rutherford B. Hayes.

The hour of their appointment came and went. However, these Paiutes gave no indication they were being kept waiting, for to the Indian time is a servant, not a master. Further, had they wanted to complain it would have been left to Sarah, the only one of the three who could easily speak the white man's tongue. And quite possibly, Sarah, alone, realized this was the white man's way of showing his superiority. She had waited in enough offices of regional Bureaus of Indian Affairs to appreciate this subtle insult. She knew the secretary's polite excuses, when he finally did receive them, would cover up a satisfaction his pallid ego might have experienced by keeping the "red dogs" waiting.

Sarah understood well enough why she, with her brother and father, had been invited to come from the Far West to the white man's eastern capital. She knew government officials considered her troublesome and a nuisance with her direct appeals to American people in asking help for her tribe.

For several months Sarah had been lecturing in California to any organization or club that would listen. Gifted with eloquence and warmth of feeling in speech, she explained to her audiences that the Indian did not want charity — only justice and things the United States government had promised him.

Attractive, intelligent and full of zeal for her cause, Sarah drew large crowds whenever she spoke. She painted a very clear picture of the predicament of Indian tribes — cheating and lies of Indian Agents, the abject poverty in which Paiutes were forced to live and worst

Chief Winnemucca

of all, day-by-day humiliations which were drowning out the voices of a proud race of people crying in the wilderness.

It mattered little to Sarah any reasons for her call to Washington. She saw in it a chance to speak with top officials of the country who had authority in Indian affairs. The opportunity delighted her. She had tried many times to enlist help of white men with political influence to improve living conditions for Paiutes and had received many promises, all of which had been quickly forgotten. Not too long before, she had sent a desperate plea direct to Secretary Schurz, but had no reply from him.

Late in 1879, following a lecture series in San Francisco, Sarah returned to Lovelock, Nevada, to visit with her father. This land, though radically changed now for Paiutes, held a special place in the Indian woman's heart for she had many memories of happy times spent there as a child. Just a few miles northeast of this western Nevada settlement, the Humboldt disappeared as a river and water spread out forming a lush meadow and tule swamp; and it was here, before the coming of emigrants, where Paiute families assembled each spring, "everything-green-time," to dig tender shoots of the cattail, gather new leaves of squaw cabbage, net ducks in marshes and hunt for eggs in knotty clumps of reeds along the shore. It was one of their customs.

As soon as the first green leaves showed in the valley, Paiute families left their winter shelters and started looking for game and growing things. Very often certain families went to the same place year after year so they would have company while hunting and gathering food.

It was a happy time for Indian children. Ones out of the cradle, yet too young to dig roots and gather vegetables with their mothers, molded animals and warriors from spongy soil and sometimes ran races through rye grass, thick and high. They picked the violet's purple blooms and yellow blossoms from ante-lope brush, then mixed them with grass fibers to wind into wreaths.

In the high desert country's blue evening light, while ducks roasted under white ashes of a campfire, Indians prepared for their busy time of hunting and food gathering which would keep them on the run until winter came again to Paiute-land. Men shredded sagebark and twisted it into string to make netting. This they used to catch birds, small animals and fish. Others made snares by tying willow rods in various ways for traps and placed them in game trails around the camp. Women busied themselves twining baskets of pliable plant shoots and grasses for they needed these to carry early spring foods and also later when gathering berries, seeds and pine nuts.

In this atmosphere of serenity, little braves practiced shooting their mud animals with bow and arrow while young girls, decorating themselves with flower wreaths, danced and sang of the beauties of nature. It was a time of peace and love and contentment.

During the 1850s things began to change. The wide valley became a favorite camping ground for pioneers traveling Humboldt Trail. Calling it "Big Meadows," emigrants tarried to feed oxen on the abundant vegetation and to cut hay to take along on their treacherous journey across the desert.

It was inevitable that cattlemen would become attracted to Big Meadows and establish ranches there. Eventually, settlers dug irrigation ditches to enlarge hayfields and the increased population upstream began to channel off water for a variety of uses. Little by little, Indians were beggared of natural resources which had always been so plentiful until now only a few bands of them remained, struggling to eke out a meager existence in the mutilated valley.

When Sarah returned from the West Coast, some of these pitifully undernourished and ragged Paiutes came to see her. She was stricken by their plight.

Natchez Winnemucca, brother of Sarah

"Oh, dear one," they begged. "Go to see our great White Father in Washington. He will help us, surely."

Sarah was not so sure, but promised them she would go. She was making preparations for a trip to the capital city when a telegram came from J.N. Haworth, special agent of the Bureau of Indian Affairs in the West. It read, "THE PRESIDENT OF THE UNITED STATES WANTS YOU, YOUR FATHER, AND BROTHER NATCHEZ, TO GO TO WASHINGTON. I AM SENT TO GO WITH YOU."

Immediately, Sarah went to her father with the message. "You must go, my child," he said to her. "And we must go with you. When great White Father in Washington hears the truth of how we are so shamefully treated, he will do right by us."

In Special Agent Haworth's company, the three Indians embarked on a journey to the East Coast by train. They were en route a week, and several times during the trip Haworth warned Sarah, "While you're in the capital city, you mustn't talk to anyone or go anywhere alone. You'll be provided with a government escort."

The first few times, Sarah didn't reply, but finally she became annoyed. "Really, Mr. Haworth, I am not afraid. When I speak, I tell the truth. I have traveled many dangerous miles in the last fifteen years. I can take care of myself."

"I'm sure you can take care of yourself, Sarah, but that is not exactly the reason," Haworth informed her. "You see, you, your father and brother are guests of the United States government and as such, you are expected to abide by President Hayes's wishes."

With a wry smile Sarah told him she understood. And she did. Because of a wave of sympathy spreading along the West Coast as a result of her lectures, Sarah knew government officials didn't want her to talk to newsmen; they were afraid of what she might say to the press.

The train pulled into Washington very late on the night before their scheduled appointment with Secretary

Schurz. By carriage, Mr. Haworth whisked the three Indians from the station directly to Tremont House. Reporters from the *Daily Post*, the *Star*, the *Critic* and several other Washington publications who had been notified of her eastern visit, were waiting to interview the popular Indian princess. They gathered around her eagerly as soon as she stepped from the vehicle.

"When's your first lecture?" one of them quickly asked.

"How long will you be here?" another called out.

Before Sarah had a chance to answer, Haworth took her elbow in a firm grip and guided her in through the lobby and upstairs. Chief Winnemucca and Natchez followed close behind.

"I'll go now," Haworth said. "Don't leave your rooms until I return in the morning."

When they were alone, Sarah walked to a window and looked out. Through heavy lace curtains she could see groups of newsmen still lingering on the cold street below.

"The government does not want me to talk," she said. "But the people want to hear me. They want to know what I have to tell."

"But you must not, my child," the old chief told her. "You must do what our great White Father wants."

"I only hope our great White Father will be different from the rest."

Next morning, after they had breakfasted in their rooms, Mr. Haworth arrived. He escorted them from the hotel to a waiting carriage, once again hurrying past groups of newsmen.

As they drove away, Sarah asked, "Are we now going to see President Hayes?"

Haworth settled back on the seat, clearing his throat in an apologetic manner. "Well, as a matter of fact, we won't get to see the president today."

Sarah frowned. "Why not?"

"We're to visit with the secretary of Interior this morning." He smiled uncertainly. "His office is in the

Sarah Winnemucca

United States Patent Building."

If Sarah thought the last bit of information a bit irrelevant, she didn't say so. Instead, she remembered it was Mr. Schurz who had not even answered her letters begging him to help the Paiutes.

"We are going to see Mr. Schurz, secretary of the Interior," she informed her father and Natchez, and then rode on in silence.

And now, as they waited, with the hour of their appointment long past, Sarah's doubts mounted even more about this trip to Washington. Would they ever get to talk with anyone who could help, and if they did, would it be the same old story of promises which would never be fulfilled?

At last, a door to Secretary Schurz's private office opened and Mr. Haworth came toward the three waiting Indians.

"Secretary Schurz will see you now," he announced with a broad smile. "Follow me, please."

Chief Winnemucca and Natchez arose and stood, straight and silent. Sarah hesitated a moment to smooth her two long braids, then got up and started toward the door.

Just before they entered the office, Haworth whispered to Sarah, "Please—be tactful."

The Indian woman, her dark eyes wide, looked up quickly. "I will speak the truth," she said, her voice clear and distinct.

Haworth put a hand on her shoulder. "Sarah—please—don't irritate the secretary."

"I will speak the truth," she repeated.

» 2

Mr. Schurz received the Paiutes with a firm and cordial handshake. Yet, to Sarah, it was a greeting which gave her an impression of haste, of eagerness to be away and about some other business which had nothing to do with them.

"Sorry to have kept you waiting," he apologized, briefly thumbing through a small black memorandum book.

Sarah assumed the book held a schedule of his appointments for the day and couldn't help but wonder why these officials, whose business was supposed to be Indian affairs, were invariably too busy with other things to take time to sit down and actually talk with a representative of the red man. Didn't they realize if it were not for her people there would be no Indian Bureau, and therefore, no jobs?

"Please, be seated," the secretary said, motioning to a long row of chairs comfortably upholstered in rich brown leather. "I'm indeed sorry my time is so limited."

As Sarah sat down she looked at Secretary Schurz

carefully. Judging from his discourteous treatment of her letters to him, she expected to see a paunchy, abominable bully of a man, but he was not like that at all. Slight of build, with sensitive features and the trained, well-modulated voice of a successful politician, he seemed mature and intelligent and extremely well-mannered.

"Did you enjoy your trip?" he asked.

"Yes, sir. It was long."

"Is this the first time you have been to Washington?" he continued.

"Yes, sir. It is far from our homeland."

"Well, well," he remarked, smiling expansively. "You must have a look at our city while you are with us."

"Sir, that is not the purpose of our visit," Sarah told him courteously but emphatically. "We have come to see the president."

"To be sure, to be sure." Secretary Schurz flushed slightly and adjusted small, gold-rimmed reading glasses on his thin nose. There was a short silence before he went on.

"Sarah, General Howard informed me you were a great help not only to him but to the other soldiers and to our country during the recent Indian uprising of the Bannock tribe in the West. I want you to know how much this Department appreciates your services."

"Thank you, sir. I did what I could," Sarah replied. "It is very hard for Indians to understand we must keep peace. I know, as do my father and my brother, that war will only destroy our race."

"Too bad those savage Bannocks didn't feel as you do. They're a rebellious lot, but we finally got them under control. They should have known better than to start a war. . . ."

Sarah stiffened slightly. "I beg to differ with you, sir," she interrupted. *"White* men start Indian Wars." She hesitated.

Although Sarah had never approved, still, deep down inside, she felt Bannocks had good reason for taking the path to war. They were starving on their Idaho reservation because the government agent confiscated all their supplies and shipped them back East to his relatives. Then, when white settlers were allowed to move in onto Camas Prairie, which ran Indians away from the only remaining food supply they had, the camas root, there was nothing for Bannocks to do but fight.

"Have you ever been hungry when there was nothing to eat, and no place to go to *get* anything to eat?" Sarah questioned.

Mr. Schurz had no answer for her. He undoubtedly realized this Indian woman's intelligence and loyalty to her race. After a moment of silence he asked, "What is it you want for your people?"

"To bring them back to Nevada," Sarah replied at once. "You sent many Paiutes far away to Yakima Reservation in Washington Territory after the Bannock War, even the ones who helped your soldiers. My people are wretched there, starving and naked, and treated like cattle or sheep. Why—oh why—did you send them there, sir?"

Sarah got up and took a step toward his desk, her hands outstretched pleadingly. "Let my brother, Lee, and all peaceful Paiutes come back to their homeland. Give them a place to live in the sage country. They have always been friends to you and to our country. Let them return to their families."

Haworth came over to touch Sarah's arm. She glanced at him, saying, "I am all right. But I also want to tell the secretary about white settlers who take our land and about Indian Agents who cheat my people and steal from them. These white men are supposed to be Christian; they look up at the sky and talk. Then they fill their pockets by selling government supplies sent for us and let Indians starve. The Paiutes want to work but your agents take everything they raise away from them." Her hands were still outstretched. "I implore you to do something." She then went back to her chair and sat down.

Schurz turned to the chief and Natchez. "Do either of you wish to say anything further?"

Chief Winnemucca arose slowly and stood erect. He spoke carefully, with sweeping gestures and great dignity. "Bring my people home. We want peace but agents cause Indians to go on warpath. White man make money off Indian Wars. Great White Father promise help if we keep peace. I keep promise. You do not. My hair is gray; I am old. Bring my son home. Bring all my people home from Yakima, now." He turned. "That is what I speak."

When Chief Winnemucca had finished, the secretary nodded thoughtfully, and then glanced at a gold watch he took from his vest pocket.

"I'm so sorry. I have no more time. I thank you for coming." He turned to Haworth. "See that our guests are taken on a tour of the city."

They walked out of the building and down broad, granite steps. Sarah moved along slowly, more than a little bewildered by such a short conference with Secretary Schurz. This time, there had been no promises which would not be kept; in fact, there had not been one word of encouragement that things would be better.

Haworth rubbed his hands together briskly. "Well, now, where would you like to go first?" he asked in a cheerful tone of voice.

"To meet President Hayes," Sarah said. *"He* is the one who invited us. *He* is the one we came to see."

"You will—you will—," Haworth snapped irritably. "But you must understand the president is a very busy man. It may be several days before he has time to see you."

"Very well. Then I will have time to give some public lectures," Sarah announced.

"No! You mustn't!"

"Why not?"

"For a number of reasons," Haworth flustered and waved for a carriage. "We'll have to eat lunch now, for we have a full afternoon of sightseeing planned."

Sarah stopped abruptly to stare at Haworth. "We did not come to Washington to see the sights."

"But—but that is what your great White Father wants you to do," Haworth replied in exasperation.

Although extremely disappointed, Sarah realized there was nothing left for them to do but go sightseeing; in fact, that is all they did for the next few days, with only two interruptions.

One came when they stopped briefly at a clothing store where Mr. Haworth bought Chief Winnemucca a suit of clothes.

"A gift from the United States government," he announced loudly, handing the ill-fitting army uniform to a clerk for disposal. But Chief Winnemucca shook his head, indicating he wished to keep his old clothing, so the clerk wrapped it for him to take along.

The other interruption of sightseeing came when Secretary Schurz summoned them for a second interview. This was no real surprise to Sarah, for she was certain Haworth informed the secretary of her intention to make some public appearances.

This time, there was no long period of waiting in the reception room of the Department of Interior. They were taken in at once and Secretary Schurz went straight to business at hand.

"So, Sarah, I understand you are bound to lecture."

"Yes, Mr. Schurz. I feel people would like to hear me."

He smiled. "Tell me, Sarah, do you think it right to speak against the United States government while you, your father and brother are its guests here in Washington?"

"Right or wrong, people should hear the truth," she said sincerely.

"You surely must realize we plan to help you with your problem." Schurz straightened, and his voice took on a more businesslike tone. "Actually, it is my feeling you can accomplish more now by going home and getting the Indians relocated on reservations. Then, later, if you need to come back for further discussion, we will pay your way here and back again."

Sarah frowned doubtfully. "Do you mean—?" she began.

"I mean we will grant all you asked for at our first meeting," he broke in. "Further, I'll give you a copy of an order which will accomplish these things. And, I'll write Agent Wilbur at Yakima Reservation this very day about releasing Paiutes who are there."

Sarah stared at him, unbelieving. "Do you speak the truth?" she asked skeptically.

Schurz got up and moved quickly around his desk. "Of course. Now, if you'll tell me where you will be located, we can send supplies directly to you and let you decide how best to issue them among the Indians." He hesitated. "You can do this, can't you?"

Sarah had recovered a little from her amazement at the words he spoke. "Oh, yes, I can—if—if the supplies come."

"They will," he assured her. "We'll ship them as soon as you get back to Nevada."

Excitedly, Sarah explained the secretary's good news to Chief Winnemucca and Natchez. They smiled and nodded their heads in happy approval. When they left, both men shook hands with Mr. Schurz and Sarah thanked him fervently.

"This will mean a lot to my people," she said, and told him she would send word as soon as she arrived in Lovelock, Nevada.

The sightseeing began again although now Sarah could take it with better grace. They were taken to the mile-long bridge across the Potomac and to the partially finished Washington Monument. They went to museums, churches, schools, hospitals and government buildings.

Only once did Sarah become angry. It was on an afternoon when they were driven past many beautiful mansions and Haworth told them they were homes of government officials.

"I am not interested in their beautiful homes," Sarah couldn't help but exclaim. "My people do not have a tent over their heads, nor blankets to cover with, nor food to eat. What do we care about seeing fine homes of people who get money to build them by stealing from the starving Indians!"

By Friday, she had stood it long enough. "I want to know the truth," she demanded of Haworth. "Are we going to see President Hayes? Yes or No!"

"Yes. You will see the president tomorrow."

That evening in their rooms, Sarah told her father and Natchez, "My mind is made up. If we do not get to see President Hayes in the morning, I am going to give an interview to the press."

Natchez shook his head in disapproval. "I do not think you should do it."

"But they are putting us off. It is what white men call 'politics'."

"I think you should wait, my daughter," Chief Winnemucca said. "Remember promises Mr. Schurz made to us. Our great White Father, the president, will see to it that promises made will come true, once we have made talk with him."

"All right," she agreed. "But I will wait only one more day."

Sarah couldn't help but wonder what the President of the United States would look like. She remembered soon after the Bannock War, her horror at hearing orders had come from the president in Washington to Fort McDermit, Nevada, for soldiers to remove peaceful Paiutes right along with prisoners of war to Yakima Reservation, far to the north beyond the Columbia River.

"It cannot be so!" she'd exclaimed. "In this cold and snow old people and little children will die. Oh, what can the president be thinking of!"

At the time she told an army officer at the fort, "I have never seen a president in my life, but I think he must be made of wood or rock, for I cannot believe a human being would do such a thing as send anyone across the fearful mountains in midwinter."

Every night for a long time afterward, Sarah dreamed of the president. He appeared as a giant bullfrog, with huge ears, big eyes, long legs and a small pointed head. Now, at last, she hoped to see how he really looked.

As Mr. Haworth had promised, on Saturday they were driven to the White House. A guide approached and told them since there would be a short wait before they could see President Hayes, a tour of the Mansion had been arranged. Sarah told him, not unkindly, they simply were not interested in seeing the Mansion. "We wish only to see the president," she said.

The three Indians were taken to the second floor, and as they approached a parlor where a small group of women waited, one came to meet them.

"I am Mrs. Hayes," she introduced herself. "When I heard you were coming, I took the liberty of inviting a few of my friends to meet you." She smiled at Sarah in a friendly manner. "They are particularly interested in meeting you, my dear. We all feel you are very brave and are touched to the heart with what you are trying to do for your people."

"This is very encouraging," Sarah replied.

After introductions, Chief Winnemucca and Natchez stood with the guide while Sarah talked with these women. She answered as many of their questions as possible and for the first time since coming to Washington sensed warmth and understanding from this small audience.

One woman moved to her side with a rustling of heavy silk. Sarah didn't know her then, of course, but regarded her as a very special person. "Keep up the noble work for your people, my dear," she said with a charming smile crinkling her eyes. "And let me give you some advice. No matter how many try to stop you, never accept defeat." She handed Sarah an engraved card.

"Write me if ever I can help," she insisted. "I love to promote a worthy cause."

Sarah glanced at the card before tucking it into her beaded bag. *"Elizabeth Palmer Peabody, Boston, Massachusetts"* it read.

"Thank you very much," she replied to the eastern woman, as the guide suggested they be on their way.

Sarah joined her father and brother as they were ushered into an oval-shaped study filled with heavy mahogany furniture. Portraits of the first five presidents hung on the walls.

"We will wait long here," Sarah predicted.

"It is all right," Chief Winnemucca told her. "Our White Father knows all or he would not have white nation. He will talk and treat us right."

"Yes," Natchez agreed. "White Father can do anything. He does not tell lies."

"I hope you are right," Sarah spoke solemnly. "Surely he will take time to talk with us."

"We will counsel long. Tell him all," the old chief concluded.

At last, a door opened. The guide stood and indicated for them to do likewise.

"The President of the United States," he announced.

President Hayes walked in hurriedly, as if he had not a minute to spare. It surprised Sarah to see he bore no resemblance at all to the ogre of her dreams. Instead, he was a distinguished-looking, middle-aged man with graying hair.

He smiled, shook hands all around and then directed a question to Sarah. "Did you get what you want for your people?"

"It has all been promised to me, sir," Sarah replied. "If I—."

"Good!"

The president nodded his head a time or two, then turned and left the room. That was the extent of an audience the three Paiutes from Nevada had with their great White Father in Washington.

On Sunday morning Sarah, Chief Winnemucca
and Natchez started their homeward journey and soon
were as far in distance as they were in understanding
of government officials who had been their hosts for
a week. Sarah had with her a copy of Secretary Schurz's
order to release Paiutes who were held on Yakima
Reservation and this made the three Indians very happy.
Still, Sarah felt doubtful. She had learned from past
experience not to believe anything in which white men
were involved until it happened. Intuition warned her
this might be just another political scheme to get her
out of Washington before she talked to newspaper
reporters or made a public appearance.
Anyway, she had met her first president and smiled,
remembering the mental picture she had of him prior
to their meeting. Sarah's imagination always had been
very active when she tried to visualize the appearance
of someone she'd never met. Even when only a
youngster as she listened to older Paiutes speak in
hushed and frightened voices about the "emigrant"
with his big white eyes and hair all over his face, in her
child's mind she thought of him looking like a big owl.
But this illusion had been over thirty years ago when
she was only a little girl.

» 3

The Indian princess was born during the early 1840s in a bark-and-tule wickiup near Nevada's Humboldt Lake and named *Thocmetony,* which means 'shell-flower'. In later years, some people called her Sadie, but she became known to America as Sarah.

In those early days Paiutes were not confined to reservations, but were free to roam the friendly sage country to their heart's content. They had a regular plan of wandering as seasons changed and spent most of the year gathering and storing food for those few cold months they had to stay in winter shelters.

Their months had no particular number of days, only a time from one new moon to the next. They knew which berries would ripen with the crescent moon, the half moon, and the full moon. They knew when every root patch must be dug, seeds gathered, when rabbits were fattest and fish spawned. Years were not counted and remembered only by an important event like a disastrous drought or snowstorm.

In deserts, valleys and mountains, young braves

hunted with bow and arrow while 'old ones' charmed the antelope and deer. Families fished in clear streams of the high country and in valley lakes of deepest blue. There were special times for gathering seeds, harvesting pine nuts and digging tender roots of herbs before tops withered away.

Indian men, young and old, worked with their hands to carve all sorts of tools and weapons from rocks or bones or the hard stems of plants. From grasses and reeds, women twined cooking utensils, watertight baskets, utility bags and winnowing trays to make their work more efficient and perhaps a little easier. For although men did the strenuous work of hunting, women did the tedious, backbreaking task of gathering in all growing things.

Using strips of fur from animals, Indians wove blankets and robes to keep themselves warm during cold weather. Fringed costumes and moccasins were made from deerskin and also from fibers of the sagebark.

Paiutes were a happy, hard-working, peace-loving people who worked together, played together and shared equally. Their life pattern was built on everyone's welfare. The Council Tent served as a meeting place and any person who had something to say was urged to speak.

One Big Chief, a title handed down from father to son, served the entire Paiute nation as leader, and sub-chiefs were appointed by him for special duties and leadership of individual tribes. Each band had complete freedom, but none had a thought for personal gain; betterment of the entire group was their primary concern. Thus, it is no wonder these Indians could not understand the many selfish motives of white men.

At Sarah's birth, Big Chief of the Paiute nation was her grandfather, Winnemucca I, a wise and diplomatic leader with a warm and loving heart. He was like a father to several thousand Indians, referring to them always as his children and seeing they had proper food, adequate clothing and comfortable homes.

He was concerned with other areas of development as well. He taught his people to always tell the truth, to love peace and do their best to keep it. He impressed upon them the importance of loving one's fellow man and insisted upon proper respect for women and tender regard for the aged and helpless.

With such kindness and trust in his heart, Big Chief was not alarmed when white settlers began to push their way into Paiute Country during the 1840s. When his people came with expressions of concern, he tried his best to calm their fears.

"Have good hearts," he told them at the Council Tent. "They are our white brothers. Make them welcome."

"It is bad," Paiutes said, shaking their heads. "We are afraid. They are not as we are."

"It is only the color of their skin that is different," Big Chief explained.

"Ah, we are afraid that is not true," many old ones insisted. "They bring much trouble."

"Listen," Sarah's grandfather said. "I must make you understand. I will tell you an old Paiute fable."

"In the beginning, the mother and father of all creation had four children—two boys and two girls. One boy and one girl were dark and the other two were white. This family lived in peace while these children were young, but as they grew older they began to quarrel, and soon were fussing and fighting constantly.

"This grieved their parents. They tried to teach the children happiness comes from understanding and sharing with one another. But their children would not listen. Eventually, the mother and father realized the four young people could not live together in peace and must be separated.

"The father who had mystic power, called his white boy and girl to him and said, 'Depart from your brother and sister. Go across the mighty ocean and do not seek each other's lives.' They obeyed and were seen no more by their heartbroken parents.

"Through the years, the dark children grew into a large nation—the one to which Paiutes belong. They always hoped descendants of the white boy and girl, who were also a great nation, would send someone to meet them so their former trouble could be settled. It was their hope the time would come when both nations could live together in peace and friendship."

Big Chief looked about with a cheerful smile at the silent Indians. "And now, the time has come!" he finished his story. "The lost children are here and we must welcome them with open arms."

It is unfortunate these 'lost children'—the prospectors and other adventurers moving westward—did not hear Big Chief's story. They were suspicious of Indians they met along their route and rebuffed any friendly gestures made by them.

Finally, a party of emigrants on horseback stopped to rest in a fertile valley on the eastern base of the Sierra Nevada. Big Chief took a group of his men and paid them a visit.

As he approached the white men's camp, Big Chief dropped his rabbit-skin robe to show he was unarmed and held out both hands in friendly greeting. The white men were impressed with his gracious manner in spite of their distrust of all Indians. They made him welcome. When he took a fancy to metal cooking utensils they were using, the white men presented him with a tin plate. He immediately made holes in it for a chin strap, put it on his head like a hat and hurried away to show his people.

In 1845, Big Chief met soldiers and explorer, John Fremont, who camped with his men near the site of present-day Wadsworth, Nevada. In his effort to make them feel welcome, the Chief repeated over and over a Paiute word, *truckee, truckee,* which means, 'it is all right.' Thinking he was telling them his name they dubbed him 'Chief Truckee' which pleased the old Indian very much and made him feel important.

Fremont, who was exploring for the United States government, accepted the chief's offer to lead his party over treacherous mountain ridges to the sunny valleys of California. En route, the men became so fond of their Indian guide they named a beautiful mountain stream which they followed up and over the Sierra Nevada *Truckee,* in his honor.

By now, Chief Truckee was considered to be trustworthy. At the outbreak of the Mexican War, he was commissioned by Fremont to serve as a scout captain and was given not only a title but also a blue uniform with shiny brass buttons, both of which he was very proud. Before he left his tribes to take over his new work for the government, he appointed his son, *Poito,* Sarah's father, to be Big Chief over all the Paiutes while he was away and extracted a promise from him to keep peace with their pale-faced brothers.

Poito, who became Winnemucca II and later called 'Old Winnemucca,' was able to keep this promise for a time, probably because the war with Mexico put a temporary halt to any westward trek. But traffic picked up again in 1849 when word of a gold strike in California flashed across the nation. There was a veritable stampede, and somewhere along the line things got out of control. Relations between Indians and whites went from good to bad, and then bad to worse, making the final chapters of the settling of the West a story not very pleasant to read.

That year in April, in "hackberry-leaves-are-out-time," before Sarah's grandfather returned from California, news came to Winnemucca II that the strangers they had been taught to call their 'white brothers' were killing every Indian who happened to get in their way. This talk spread fast through spring camps. Paiutes were terrified.

"We must save our children," they cried to each other. "The 'white brothers' must not kill our children."

Sarah's father, heavy of heart and with no time for pondering over a solution, gave a command. "March to the mountains. Keep out of sight and stay in high country. There will be roots and berries and later many pine nuts to gather. We can store supplies for the coming cold time. If white man leave, we can hunt streams and lakes for fish to dry. Young braves will go into valleys to hunt. We can live in the mountains for many moons."

No time could be lost. Paiutes hurriedly left their camps carrying water jugs, baskets and babies on their backs. Once in the comparative safety of high country, they got to work gathering food for winter. Women and children dug roots, gathered seeds and later harvested pine nuts. For skins and meat men flooded holes of small animals and hunted other game in the forests.

When winter came to the mountains, slowing emigrant wagon traffic, Indians ventured down to Humboldt River to fish, to dig more roots and gather more seeds and berries of shrubs covering the valley floor.

Of course they had no time to store the food supply in their usual careful way. Instead of digging a deep pit in which to place provisions and then carefully concealing it with earth, they piled the reserve in a huge cone-shaped mound resembling a wigwam to an extent, and covered it over with grasses and mud.

Unfortunately, they left this pile of winter stores too close to a traveled route and a group of whites passing by set it afire.

From high rocky ridges, Paiutes watched in horror as their food for the winter burned. The fire flared, sputtered, crackled and caught again, and then a wind picked up flames which swirled and writhed and danced like venomous serpents leaping toward the desert sky. Sarah, even though only a small child at the time, never forgot this senselessly cruel act of the white men.

When Chief Truckee returned home late that fall, he simply refused to believe his white brothers had deliberately destroyed the supply of food.

"Do not have dark hearts," he implored his people.

"We must forgive them."

"How can we forgive?" Indians cried in anguish. "Already there is snow on mountains and in valleys and no way to get more food. We will starve. Oh, why did they do it?"

"They know not what they do," the old chief said, unaware he was quoting the white man's Bible.

The following spring, emigrants living at Humboldt Sink committed another act of violence against Indians. A group of braves fishing in the river were fired on, and five of them were killed. Paiutes held council after council, trying to get their chief's permission to go back and take revenge on the murdering white men, but the old Indian chief would not consent.

"They killed in fear, not in anger," he insisted. "They are our brothers and belong to a mighty nation. There must never be war between us."

All that year they spent in the mountains, Chief Truckee tried very hard to bring about a better understanding of whites by his people. In the evening, he would sit cross-legged before a campfire, telling many wonderful stories of things he had seen in California. He told about his white brothers' big houses, schools they had for their children and the beautiful clothes they wore. He even taught his people to sing some soldiers' roll calls and "The Star-Spangled Banner."

His stories were fascinating to Sarah. Next to her mother and father, she loved most her kindly grandfather who liked to swing her high into the air and call her his sweetheart. Very often, she would get the storytelling started by saying, "Dear grandfather, tell us about the *ways* of white people."

"What does my sweetheart want to hear?" he would ask.

"About a house that walks on water," would come the shy answer.

Then the old man, with a pleased look, would draw his circle of listeners nearer and with a red glow of the campfire on his face, would begin. "It can travel faster than any horse in the world. It makes a noise they call 'whistle'—a beautiful noise, and there is another noise called 'bell.' It is a big house that walks all over the mighty ocean."

"How big?" Sarah would ask quickly.

Then the chief, through squinted eyes, would look far away across the desert, past sandy basins, grassy valleys and jagged ridges to shadowy outlines in the far distance. "As big as that hill you see over there," he would point out. "And as high as that mountain."

"Oh, that cannot be possible!" his amazed listeners would exclaim. "It cannot be true!"

"It is true, every word of it," the chief declared. "And that is nothing to what I am going to tell you. Our white brothers are a mighty people. They have a gun that can shoot a ball bigger than my head. It can go as far away as the mountains over there."

Then, he proudly showed them a piece of paper Fremont had given him. On it was written,

Truckee is a trustworthy friend of the white people. I urge you to treat him as such. John C. Fremont.

The old chief called the piece of paper his 'rag friend.' "This can talk for us to all our white brothers and sisters and their children," he explained. "Our white brothers can talk to each other on paper."

Indians couldn't believe it. They shook their heads. "Then, they cannot be truly human. They must be pure spirits."

All winter Chief Truckee continued to tell his wonderful stories about white people. When spring came, he announced to the Indians he wanted to take thirty Paiute families with him to California as soon as snow left the mountains.

"Then, in that way, you will know what I say is truth."

30]

» 4

Sarah did not want to go to California. She loved to listen to her grandfather's fascinating stories about white people, but it was her sincere desire to stay just as far away from them as possible. She'd heard too much talk among 'old ones' that these white strangers ate Indian children.

However, very few Paiutes had been beyond the Sierra Nevada and Big Chief felt the time had come for more of them to get out and see the world. Among the thirty families chosen by him to start for California in the summer were Sarah, her mother, and brothers Tom and Natchez, and her sisters Elma and Mary. Her father, Winnemucca II, would have to stay with the tribes at home.

As time drew near, Sarah became frightened. "Oh, grandfather, please do not take me to California," she begged. "I do not wish to leave my dear father."

The old man picked her up and held her in his arms. "Little Shellflower, you are my sweetheart," he told her. "I want you to see my good white brothers, and I want them to see you."

"No! No!" Sarah protested, beginning to cry. "I don't want to see them! Not the owls! Please, Grandfather, not the owls!"

Even Sarah's mother begged to remain at home. She wanted to be with her husband, but the old chief insisted she go. He talked and talked, trying to convince Paiutes it would be a wonderful experience for them, but it was not until he promised to bring them back when the "green-grass-growing-fast-time" came again that they agreed to go.

"What if we catch up with houses on wheels?" Sarah asked her mother. "They are rolling through our land all of the time."

"Do not be afraid, my child. Grandfather told me his 'rag friend' will talk for him and keep us all safe."

The day before they left, women gathered food for celebrating the departure and that night they feasted on choke-berries and refreshing drinks made from wild rose stems and sage leaves. Everyone sang travel songs, danced and prayed to their spirit father for a safe journey. They wept, too, because of the coming long separation from loved ones.

When it came time to go, Sarah clung to her father. "I do not want to leave you," she cried. "Come with us to California."

Winnemucca held his daughter close. "It is good for you to go. Do as your grandfather wishes, dear child. He is wise and will protect you."

That morning, as the first pinkish rays of a rising sun streaked the desert sky, thirty Paiute families started for an unknown land beyond the Sierra Nevada. Indian scouts headed the procession, followed by Chief Truckee and his men, sitting straight and sure on their mounts. Families came next, with children riding behind grownups and babies tied in baskets to their mothers' backs. Each Indian was dressed in his own way with bits of feathers, rabbit toes and rattling deerhoofs trimming buckskin and sagebark clothing.

Ponies were adorned with cedar sprigs and bright flowers fastened to their manes and tails.

The first day out was uneventful. That night they camped at Carson Sink. On the next day, scouts came riding back with news of 'houses on wheels' halted just ahead. The chief told his people to stay where they were while he went to talk with the emigrants.

He came back soon, his face wreathed with smiles. The white people had given him some hard bread which he divided among his Paiutes. Even Sarah had to admit it was very good.

"My 'rag friend' talked for me," he said. "As long as I live and I keep this paper which the great soldier Fremont gave me, we shall be safe." He held his paper up and kissed it. "So, my children, get your horses ready and we will move on and camp with our white brothers tonight." He looked at Sarah. "I have a little sweetheart who is much in fear of my white brothers. I want her to know how good and kind they are."

At these words, Sarah flew into a tantrum, very much like those of spoiled children in our modern day. She screamed and cried and jumped up and down, not behaving like an Indian child at all. Finally, she wrapped her rabbit-skin robe around her, even concealing her head, so she couldn't see anyone, nor they her.

Sarah's mother watched this display of temperament, an expression of worry on her gentle face. She went to the old chief and said, "I do not know what is the matter with my child, but I beg you not to stop near any white people's camp. She will surely die of fright if you do."

The old chief was also concerned for his grandchild who meant so much to him, so he gave an order to pass on by the halted white train. Sarah did not know when they passed because she rode behind her brother, Natchez, and kept wrapped in her robe.

On the third night, as they approached low foothills of the Sierra Nevada, there was no place to camp other than near white people because wagon trains were strung out all along the Carson River.

Emigrants found this a great resting spot to prepare for their long haul over the mountains. It provided water for thirsty oxen and the rich, fertile valley furnished an abundance of food. Women took advantage of the clear stream to do long overdue washings and acres and acres of sagebrush offered ample places for hanging wet things out to dry.

The Indians stopped some distance away and Chief Truckee told his people, "Never take anything from our white brothers unless they give it to you. Just because they hang their clothes outdoors does not mean they have thrown them away." He then went to the nearest camp with his 'rag friend' and returned shortly with more hard bread. Three of the white men came back with him.

At the sound of strange voices, Sarah took one quick peek through a tiny hole in her rabbit-skin robe. "The owls! The owls! Send them away!" she shrieked. "Please, grandfather, send them away."

The old chief went to the little girl and took her in his strong arms. "Don't be afraid, sweetheart," he murmured. "You surely know I will not let anything harm you."

His voice had a strange pleading note in it as though he were begging. With her head snuggled in the warm protection of his shoulder, Sarah took another look at the white visitors, only to jerk the robe even tighter over her head. Sighing, the chief gave his granddaughter to her mother and went to speak with his white friends.

As the emigrants left to return to their own camp, Sarah moved the cover enough to watch them leave. The men really didn't resemble owls. She hardly knew what they did look like. Nothing she had ever encountered before in her young life. But she had been taught, as all Indian children were, to be kind to those who did her no harm. She began to wonder if she should try harder to make friends with the strange creatures her grandfather seemed to like so much.

"Chief Truckee Spread Out his Arms as a Sign of Peace,"
an illustration by George Varian, from *Famous Indian Chiefs
I Have Known* by O.O. Howard, published in 1912.

In the cool of the evening when these white men returned, bringing their wives with them, Sarah summoned all her courage and did not hide beneath her robe. One of the women approached, holding out something in her hand.

"Take it, my child," her grandfather prompted.

Hanging to her mother's skirt with one hand, Sarah took the proffered gift with the other, and found it to be *Peharbe,* or "sugar."

The same woman presented Chief Truckee with a small tin cup. After the visitors had returned to their own camp, he gave the cup to Sarah, explaining, "When you want to drink water, put it in this cup and drink. That is the way our white friends do."

Then, he went on to tell his granddaughter about the time his white brothers had given him a tin plate. "I wore it on top of my head like feathers," he said, laughing heartily at himself. "I did not know it was intended to eat from, and wore it in our first fight with the Mexicans. My white brothers made fun of me, but it was in friendship and I laughed with them."

That night under a starlit sky, campfires flickered merrily all along the banks of Carson River and sweet music drifted through the clear Nevada air. To Sarah, these white people sounded happy. When she recalled all the good things her grandfather had told her about them she decided, "I will try to make friends with them— maybe—sometime."

The Indians traveled on up and over the Sierra Nevada and at last reached beautiful Sacramento Valley. One of the first things the chief showed his people was a big stone house on a high hill where one of his friends lived.

"It is so big you have to climb up three times before you get to the top," he said.

"We have never seen anything like it," they exclaimed, properly impressed.

He told them later, "If you listen carefully, you will hear a bell of the wonderful house that walks on water."

Sure enough, one evening in the afterglow of a setting sun, a clear "ding-dong, ding-dong, ding-dong" rang through the quiet of the night. Everyone stopped to listen and agreed it was one of the prettiest noises they had ever heard.

On the day they went to see this wonderful house, Sarah did not go because of white people she might see. Instead, she asked her brother Natchez to tell her all about it.

"The water-house has many looking glasses all around it," he told her. "And when it walked close to the land it was so tired. It breathed so loud it almost made us deaf to hear it."

In spite of the wonderful things they saw in California and kindness shown them by the old chief's many white friends, Paiutes looked forward to the time when snow would leave the mountains so they could go back to their homes and be reunited with ones they'd left behind. True to his promise, Chief Truckee started back toward Nevada with them in the spring.

As they were coming down the Sierra Nevada's eastern slope, they met a group of Indian braves bearing bad news. "Many Paiutes living along Humboldt River are dead of a strange illness," they reported.

"My son—is he dead?" Chief Truckee asked at once.

"No, he has been in the mountains and all who were there with him have been spared. It is only ones along the river."

"Go and tell our people we are coming," the chief said. "Spread word to Paiutes to come and meet us. We will wait here."

The little cavalcade camped at Genoa for a time and grieved. Men and women cut their hair and slashed their arms in mourning for loved ones who had gone to the Spirit-land while they had been away.

Within a few days, Winnemucca and his band arrived. It was a time of mingled sadness and joy, with the reuniting of families and sharing of grief. Sarah ran to her father, threw her arms around his neck and

[37

hugged him tight. Winnemucca wept tears of joy to see his beloved family once again.

Members of the tribe who had remained at home hung their heads and wept silently as they told in detail of this terrible thing which had happened.

"White people poisoned the river water," a spokesman said positively. "As soon as Indians drank of the water, they died right off. Our spirit-doctors tried to cure them, but they, too, died while trying to make others well. The water was poisoned!"

"This cannot be so," the old chief declared, shaking his head. "If our white brothers poisoned the Humboldt water, then they, too, would have died when they drank. No, my children, it must be some disease unknown to us. We must not blame our white brothers."

Many changes had taken place in Paiute country during Sarah's absence. There were new settlements all along the Egan and Humboldt River trails and many pioneers had set up business establishments.

On Carson River, where prospectors had found flakes of precious metal in a place they called Gold Canyon, a man named James Williams had built a trading station. And in Carson Valley, Salt Lake City merchant John Reese managed a branch of his large city store. He operated a sawmill and gristmill there, too.

When silver was discovered, even more miners and adventurers swarmed into Nevada, straggling through deep canyons and over craggy mountains. In Eagle Valley, Abraham Curry staked lots for a town he'd already named for Kit Carson, one of the area's first trappers. Major William Ormsby, agent for the Pioneer Stage Company, took an active part in promoting the new city of Carson.

By this time, Sarah, though no longer afraid of white men, did not like or trust them with the wholeheartedness of her grandfather. She mingled with them as little as possible, preferring the company of her own people.

When Sarah reached her teens, Chief Truckee decided she and her sister, Elma, should learn from settlers who were continuously moving in. He arranged for the two girls to live for awhile in Genoa with Major and Mrs. Ormsby.

The Ormsbys had a daughter of their own, and she became a good friend to Sarah and Elma. They studied history books and the Bible and the two Indian girls learned to speak English and some Spanish. Mrs. Ormsby even taught them to sing "The Star-Spangled Banner" and they realized it didn't sound one bit the way it had when their grandfather had sung it.

Sarah liked the Ormsbys very much; in fact, she liked most white people she met while in Genoa. She liked the clothes white people wore, the food they ate and the homes in which they lived. It was their "ways" that puzzled her and caused her to have mixed emotions regarding them. It seemed to her they tended to jump to conclusions and panicked easily. They never took time to reason things out. But Sarah managed to adjust to things she couldn't understand and was content to stay among the white people for a time, until a tragic incident occurred.

Two settlers who were en route to California, carrying large sums of money, were murdered and robbed just outside of town. Citizens, including Major Ormsby, were positive this crime was the work of Indians because two arrows of the type used by the Washoe tribe were found sticking in both dead bodies.

A vigilante committee was quickly organized. They confronted the old Washoe chief with a demand for two Indians to pay for the lives of the murdered men.

"Washoe Indians could not have done it," the old leader told them. "None of my tribe has been away from Pinenut Valley for a long time."

"These men were killed with Washoe arrows," the committee persisted. "Bring us two of your braves."

Finally, the Washoe chief brought in two of his men because he was afraid that if he did not obey, dreadful things would be done to all his people. One of the prisoners had a wife and the other had an old mother who came along with him. Both women threw themselves at the white men's feet, weeping and begging for mercy.

"Our men have good hearts," they declared. "They did not kill. They have not been away from camp." Both women directed their pleas to Major Ormsby in particular. "You are a kind chieftain. Please believe what we say is true."

In spite of this, the two Indians were handcuffed and locked in a small building that night. Next morning, a large crowd of curious people gathered outside to see the prisoners.

"Hang the red devils!" some of them yelled.

Young boys threw stones at them and jeered and stuck out their tongues. The Indians endured it stolidly.

By afternoon, thirty-one white men, armed with guns, came to take these Indians to California to put them in jail. The grief-stricken Washoe women cried and begged, reaching out with their hands to white people. "Do not kill them! They have done nothing bad! They could not have done it. They have been in camp."

But no one would listen.

Sarah was terribly upset. Sobbing, she ran to Mrs. Ormsby. "I believe those Indians," she cried. "They are telling the truth. Please, tell your husband they did not kill those two white men."

"Then how did their arrows get in the bodies?" Mrs. Ormsby asked, with no sympathy in her voice. "Besides, my husband knows what he is doing."

Sarah ran back as some white men removed the Indian prisoners. Washoe women tried to get to their men, weeping and begging for mercy, but they were restrained. As soon as the Indians were in the open, they broke and ran and were shot in the back.

Although she tried, Sarah could not erase this brutal scene from her mind and even dreamed about it at night. When she learned her sister, Elma, felt the same as she did, she went to Mrs. Ormsby and said, "We want to go home to our own people."

Later, it was learned the Indians really were innocent of any wrongdoing. White men who committed the crime had put arrows in the wounds to throw suspicion on Washoes. By the time they confessed, it was too late to save the prisoners.

Already depressed by this incident, Sarah's grief became almost unbearable when she reached home and found her grandfather seriously ill. She stayed by him constantly, but all too soon the old chief called his son and spoke to him for the last time.

"Never forget your duty to your own people," he said to Winnemucca II, his voice weak and husky. "And always love and be kind to your white brothers."

Then, he turned to Sarah and took her small hand in his. "Sweetheart, do not forget my white brothers. Try to understand their 'ways.' Be kind to them and they will be kind to you and teach you many things."

Later, on that cold winter night, fires flickered on every mountain top in Paiute-land, signaling to Indians the death of their beloved Big Chief. To Sarah, his loss was a crushing blow, of more significance than the loss of a loved one. Wise beyond her years, she was already aware her people needed his kind of leadership, more now than before. Chief Truckee would be missed by Indians and white men alike.

» 5

Before Chief Truckee's death, he made arrangements through one of his good white brothers for Sarah and Elma to go to California and start their education among white people. This is why, when the warm winds came again, Sarah found herself once more on a trail to the West, accompanied by her brothers Natchez and Tom with three other Paiute braves. It was the spring of 1860.

The small band rode to the Sisters' School in San Jose. A chill wind blew sharply and rolling storm clouds reminded both girls of silvery, gray-green sage back in their home country. The school was a grand stone building which stood quiet and alone on a rise of ground overlooking beautiful Santa Clara Valley. Its size was a little overwhelming.

"I am sick for our home," Elma said to Sarah as they approached the school. "My heart is heavy, nearly to my heels. I do not think I want to stay."

"We must," Sarah told her. "This is the way our grandfather wanted it, and he was a wise man."

Nevertheless, both blinked back stinging tears when time came to tell their brothers goodbye, and they felt even worse as the Indians turned their mounts to leave. A kind-faced Sister stood at the school's entrance to take them in.

The girls were dressed alike in simple, one-piece garments with wing sleeves and fringe trim made of natural deerskin. Their hair, brushed smooth, was parted in the middle and braided into two thick plaits tied at the ends with ribbons made from twisted bark of the sagebrush. On their feet were soft-soled moccasins.

Although they made a charming picture in native costume, the Sister showed them plain gray calico dresses and high-buttoned shoes in the closet of their quarters. "When you have changed, come to talk with me," she said and then went out, closing the door.

Their room was small, but neat and attractive with white sheets and a flower-garden quilt on the bed. There was a dresser with large drawers in which they could keep personal belongings. "It's like our room at Ormsbys," Sarah exclaimed happily.

They found the Sister's office and she spoke with them briefly concerning rules and other requirements. Then, she took them to a classroom where girls ranging in ages from ten to eighteen sat on benches at both sides of long tables. They had books open and were writing on paper, but every one of them looked up when the Paiute girls entered.

"Why do they keep looking straight into your eyes?" Elma asked at recreation time.

"I suppose they do not know better," Sarah explained. "They have not been taught, as we have, it is not the proper thing to do."

The first few days were strange ones, but the Indian girls soon learned rules and became accustomed to school routine. Both were careful with books and studied conscientiously. Even after class hours, in their room, they often read aloud to each other. And although there were times of homesickness for the sage country, both liked school and were making a good adjustment to this new environment.

In the beginning, the other girls were very friendly and often coaxed Sarah and Elma to say a few words to them in Paiute language. As days passed, however, everything changed. Little by little their white classmates avoided them and soon Sarah and Elma were openly shunned. The two Indian girls stayed close together, their hearts saddened as students who had been so kind and friendly a few short days before now gathered in groups to talk to each other in muted voices.

The Paiute girls couldn't understand why until Sarah overheard whisperings about mothers and fathers saying it was a disgrace to associate with Indians. Realizing this, Elma couldn't help but cry.

"It's another one of their 'ways,' " Sarah told her. "They have not been taught to be kind to everyone as we have. Maybe they will change when they get to know us better. Time will tell."

However, Sarah and Elma didn't get to stay long enough to find out. School authorities sent word to Chief Winnemucca to have someone come for them at the end of the third week, because wealthy parents of other students objected to their daughters mingling with Indians.

Sisters at the school were very sad to lose the two girls as students. They tried to make amends for the expulsion and urged them to keep on with their studies as best they could. And even though the Indian girls were glad to be back with their own people, the incident left a bitterness in Sarah's heart. "Someday, dear Elma," she confided, "I am going to have a school—just for Indians."

With deep determination, Sarah continued learning to speak and write English through association with white settlers in whose homes she worked. Usually, she spent the small amount earned on books and through her own efforts became a well educated person.

Upon her return home from school, Sarah found the Paiutes trying hard to tolerate white people, but resentment and hatred were rapidly taking hold. Their beautiful land was being usurped; fish in the rivers and lakes had almost disappeared, and wildlife on which they depended for food and clothing had been driven away. A good part of natural resources such as seeds, roots and berries had been depleted by waste and carelessness. Indians had been pushed back and back and back, and now that miners were everywhere in the mountains, there was no place left in the sage country for them to go.

In May of that year, two young Paiute girls were kidnapped by white men who lived with James Williams at his station on the Carson River. Indians looked everywhere, through mountains and valleys, forests and canyons, following white men's trails in search of the little girls. Eventually, they found them bound and gagged, in pitiful condition, in a cold, dark cellar of the Williams station.

Wild with grief and anger, Indian braves killed the two white men responsible and set fire to the building. News spread quickly among settlers that the "red dogs" were on the warpath. No one stopped to find out why Indians who had been peaceful and quiet only a few days before would commit such a terrible act. Word was that bloodthirsty savages had murdered two hard-working, kind-hearted settlers. Fright turned to hysteria among women and uncontrollable anger among men who vowed they'd "show those damned 'red devils' a thing or two."

While the whites were making frantic preparations to wreak their revenge, Winnemucca II, now Big Chief of the Paiutes, gathered his men together, quietly and efficiently, in the region of Pyramid Lake for a council, in an effort to try to keep peace. With typical impulsiveness and loosely organized, white men charged headlong into the encampment, realizing too late they were greatly outnumbered by Indians. To protect themselves, the Indians fought back, and soon it was a matter of every man for himself.

As Natchez led a group of whooping warriors through a narrow canyon, he recognized his friend, Major Ormsby, among some trapped whites. The Major threw down his arms and begged Natchez not to kill him.

"Hurry! Drop as dead!" Natchez yelled. "I shoot over you."

Unfortunately, in all the mad, scrambling commotion and confusion, the white man failed to move quick enough. Another Paiute's perfect aim got him, and Major Ormsby fell dead.

After the humiliating defeat, white settlers sent for military help. In a few weeks, their ranks were enlarged by soldiers who organized and disciplined the group. They made a second march on the Indians, and the Paiutes, greatly outnumbered this time, soon retreated into the mountains. Here, young braves spoke of retaliation, but Winnemucca discouraged them. Perhaps because of his promise to Chief Truckee, but undoubtedly because he realized the superior power of the white nation.

This short but bloody encounter between white men and Indians had far-reaching effects. The government built a small army base, Fort Churchill, near Carson River and other forts were established in the immediate area, including Fort McDermit to the north and Harney in southeast Oregon territory. These garrisons were built as a precaution against future Indian attacks and the main duty of men stationed in them was to protect settlers. Yet, within a very few years as military men really came to know the Indians, the forts became a haven for red men, and American soldiers turned out to be their friends and protectors.

The government also set aside land for Indians in what they called Nevada, for this sage country had become a Territory with statehood just around the corner. The largest area was Pyramid Lake Reservation

Pyramid Lake on Pyramid Lake Reservation

which was sixty miles long and fifteen miles wide. It included two lakes and a timber reserve of twenty thousand acres.

To Indians who agreed to live on reservations, the government promised help. Beef, flour and blankets were to be main items supplied regularly, but they were also to get clothing, wagons, horses and tools. The head of each family was to be given a parcel of land for his own use, and officials, to be appointed by the government, would be in charge to work with the Indians, teach them to farm and do other things to improve living conditions. This would have been a wonderful solution to the problem faced by Paiutes, if the government had only kept its promises. But, of course, it didn't.

During these years, Sarah lived in the new mining town of Virginia City where she worked as a day maid in the homes of white people. She lived in a rented room and took in washings to make extra money with which to buy books. She was very clever with needle and thread, designing and making elegant shawls and beaded shirtwaists from imported silks, satins, wools and fine cotton materials brought to her by wives and daughters of wealthy miners. She made herself some dark riding skirts and bright blouses, in a style white women wore, for she liked to dress as they did.

White women who lived in this mining town found the Indian princess to be charming and invited her to their homes. Occasionally, they took her with them to special entertainments at Piper's Opera House and to dances at the Ivy Social Club.

Although Sarah enjoyed living in Virginia City and valued the many friendships made, she still went to see her own people at Pyramid Lake Reservation and became more disturbed with each visit at what she saw taking place there.

Paiutes had lost the right to govern their own affairs, and with the loss of their independence they were beginning to lose initiative as well. Settlers had moved in to take some of the land that was supposed to belong

Army officers in front of headquarters at Fort McDermit

A Northern Paiute settlement near Virginia City, Nevada, 1891

to Indians and the Central Pacific Railroad had sent crews to lay steel rails through their forests, cutting the reservation in two. Great herds of cattle which grazed on Indian land belonged to white settlers. Indians had none. The agent had not taught them to farm; indeed, none of the Indians had any farm land to call their own. A few of them worked for the agent and were paid a dollar a day. But this pittance had to be used to buy supplies which had been sent by the government to be rationed, free of charge, to inhabitants of the reservation. Those with no money scoured wastelands for what vegetation and insects they could find to eat. Many were dying of starvation.

Some settlers in surrounding areas had written to the commanding officer at Fort McDermit, relating the pathetic condition of these Indians. This was not so much because they cared for red men, but more because they feared an uprising if something were not done for them soon.

At last Sarah, who was now a lovely young woman in her twenties, could stand it no longer. In 1866, she left Virginia City and returned to her people. They needed her.

Natchez and Tom were the only members of Sarah's immediate family left at Pyramid. Her mother and sister Mary had died. Elma was living with a white family in Montana. Two younger sisters were gone and a baby brother had been killed. Chief Winnemucca had taken four hundred of his people north into the Oregon mountains, and a young brother, Lee, growing into a handsome young brave, had gone with his father.

Sarah went at once to the agent, the seventh one who had been at Pyramid in six years, and a person she detested. He was a man small in stature who, typically, tried to make up for it by flaunting authority and talking vulgar, especially to Indians.

"What in hell do you want?" he roughly asked Sarah as she entered his office.

"I have come to help my people," she replied. "I

will live here now."

The agent's eyes narrowed. "Well, let's get one thing straight then, right off. I don't want you meddlin' in any reservation business."

Sarah's dark eyes grew wide and all but flashed fire. "It is *our* reservation, *not yours!*" she couldn't help but tell him.

She had been back only a short time when a crisis arose. The agent sold one of her tribe some gunpowder, which was certainly against the law. Then, a government employee shot this Indian because of his unlawful possession of an explosive.

News of a murder spread fast among Paiutes and soon, runners came flying to tell Sarah of a gathering of tribes to plan an attack on Agency headquarters that very night.

Although in her heart, Sarah could not blame Indians for feeling as they did, she knew such an attack would only make matters worse. She ran to get Natchez. They jumped on their horses and hurried to the agent's quarters to warn him.

"You must go away, quickly," Sarah told him. "My people are coming to kill you. Those who live along the river will not be safe either."

The agent laughed in an insulting way. "I'm not afraid. Let your people come. We have a good many guns here. We'll show the damn' red devils how to fight."

"No! You don't have to be afraid," Sarah exclaimed. "You can kill Indians, even shoot them in the back and nothing will be done to you. Not so with Indians. If they kill a white man, it is the end of them."

"The sooner all Indians are done for, the better it will be."

Sarah fought down her anger and begged once more. "Please, leave now. We don't want our people to get in trouble."

"Get out of here!" he ordered. "And why don't the both of you get clear off this reservation? You're the

[51

ones who cause trouble."

Sarah realized the futility of trying to reason with the Agent. She sent Natchez galloping upriver to warn settlers and she went back to Paiutes who were waiting uneasily around their camps. Before midnight her brother returned at so fast a pace his horse nearly fell beneath him. Sarah ran to meet him.

"What has happened?" she cried, fearful at the look on his face. Frightened Indian men, women and children gathered around them.

"I had a vision," he told her breathlessly. "It came before me in a fog rising from the river. I saw it happen!"

"What happened?" cried Sarah. "What?"

"It is true our people planned to kill, but not the agent! They went to Deep Wells and the deed is already done." He hesitated. "I saw only one dead, but another will die soon."

Natchez looked as if in a daze and shook his head slightly. "It is only a vision, my sister, but it is true. We must go and do what we can to help."

Egan, a peace-loving and influential chief, came over to talk with Natchez and soon, with thirty braves, they rode away toward Deep Wells. Sarah waited for them all through the chill of the night. At last, in the cold, gray dawn she saw a brave coming, riding fast. She hurried to meet him.

"The news is bad. We shall all die this very day," he told her, speaking with haste.

Sarah tried to calm the excited young man. "Tell me everything that happened," she urged.

"Two white men have been killed—at Deep Wells. Indians did it!"

"Oh-h-h!" Paiutes moaned. "The vision is true!"

"Did you see them?" Sarah asked.

"Yes, and that is not all I have to tell. Our agent has gone to get soldiers to come and kill us all! I saw him on the way to soldiers' camp—riding fast."

Paiutes wept bitterly, in grief and fear. "Soldiers are coming to kill us," they kept repeating and moaning.

Sarah tried to comfort them, but even she felt a dark foreboding of the future.

In the early afternoon, two Indian scouts brought Sarah a letter. It was from U.S. army officer, Captain Jerome, and it read:

> Miss Sarah Winnemucca,
> Your agent tells us very bad things about your people. I would like to speak with you and your brother Natchez at your place. Please reply.
>
> > Captain Jerome
> > Fort McDermit.

The scouts waited for Sarah's answer, but she had nothing with which to write. She looked around. "Bring me a stick with a sharp point," she told one of the children, and to a woman said, "And some fish's blood."

With this contrivance, she wrote on the back of Captain Jerome's letter:

> My brother and I will be waiting for you at my camp.
>
> > Sarah Winnemucca.

Immediately after the scouts left, frightened Paiutes gathered around Sarah to find out what the message meant. She didn't want to tell them soldiers would arrive, but still it would be better for them to know they were coming to talk instead of to kill. At least, Sarah hoped it would be that way. Yet, her distrust of white men sent little shudders of doubt through her own mind.

Taking a deep breath, she spoke calmly to the Paiutes. "Do not be afraid. Soldiers are coming to talk. We shall wait for them."

At her words, Indians broke into a great wailing. "Oh, spirit-father, help us," they uttered. "Soldiers are coming to kill us!"

» 6

Time all but stood still through the dark hours while Paiutes waited for the soldiers. Sarah did her best to encourage those in scattered lodges and ones who congregated around her own camp. But in truth, she scarcely knew what to expect from her first direct encounter with the military.

Then, at last, breaking a hollow, empty silence of desert wilderness came the fast, muffled thud of many horses' hooves, and a cavalry division from Fort Mc-Dermit rode in through the night. At first, Indians grew very still, as if paralyzed, but as horses appeared, they clutched one another, sobbing with fear.

A tall, lean man with a thin, lined face swung down from his horse and walked over to Sarah, who was standing, straight and proud, a little in front of her terrified people. He saluted her, and then said, in a deep voice, "We have come to help. Tell your people not to be afraid."

"I have been telling them that all night long," she said, her voice steady and clear, "but they have a deep fear of men in uniform—and for good reason."

"Do you mind telling me why, ma'am?" he asked with concern.

"I will tell you. At Muddy Lake, over two years ago, many of my people were fishing, bothering no one. A company of soldiers came by and fired into the camp with their wagon guns, killing nearly everyone—blowing them to pieces. The few who got away came back later to try to help any wounded, but by then, white men had set fire to the encampment. They threw tiny babies still tied in their cradles into the flames and watched them burn alive—my own baby brother." Sarah's voice had dropped lower now.

"I see." The soldier was thoughtful, his eyes full of sorrow. "Were any more of your family killed?"

"The camp was mostly old men and women and children. My father had taken young men to Carson Sink on a hunting excursion and my mother had gone to the river to pick ripe buckberries. My baby brother was in the care of grandmother—and she was killed, too." Sarah's eyes misted over with tears, but her head was still high and proud. "My poor, dear father was bowed down with grief, and still—and still—he kept peace with your people."

"Where is your father now, ma'am?" he asked.

"He has gone north to the mountains, far away from white men. He said he would live out his life there."

"I have heard a great many good things about your father and also your grandfather, Chief Truckee. He was a fine, wise man."

Sarah smiled, but it was tinged with despair. "I loved my grandfather dearly," she said. "But I do not know that he was wise to raise his hand in welcome to your people. It has not been worth what we have suffered."

Captain Jerome took a step toward her, his face intense with desire to win her trust. "Please believe me when I tell you those men at Muddy Lake were not true soldiers. They were only some men trying to stir up trouble out here to keep from having to go to the big war down South—the War between the States. Tell your people that, for me, Sarah. Tell them real soldiers are like we are, and not to believe those other men were soldiers, even if they were in uniform. We don't want to harm your people. We want to help them."

Sarah looked at him for a long moment. She could not doubt the sincerity expressed in every line of his face and in his clear blue eyes.

"Yes, I will tell them."

She turned to Indians clinging to one another around the campfire and spoke a few words. They became quiet and listened. Then, Sarah told them what Captain Jerome had said about the men at Muddy Lake.

"I believe what this Captain Jerome says is truth," she finished. "I think he wants to help us."

"It is all right now," Sarah said, turning back to the captain with a slight smile. "If you tell truth, they will trust you."

"It's you they trust, Sarah—not me," he told her, a look of pure admiration in his eyes for the Indian princess. "And I trust you, too. Now, will you tell me what started the trouble here? I have only the agent's side of the story."

"I have no idea what he told you, but the truth is he sold an Indian some gunpowder, and then one of his men shot the poor man because he had it," Sarah replied mater-of-factly.

"That goddam' son-of-a-bitch," Captain Jerome murmured under his breath. "You mean. . . ."

"The agent didn't care; it was just more money in his pocket," Sarah broke in. "He is not concerned about us."

The captain looked around, scanning groups of Indians huddled together who were still staring at him somewhat doubtfully. "Your people are in a pathetic condition. Do they have anything at all to eat?"

"Very little. We will have more soon, when it is 'fish-run-up-the-river-time.' "

"But you need something now," he reflected. "I'll

take a couple of men back to the fort with me and send some supplies. I'd better leave the rest of the soldiers here. Lieutenant Bartlett will be in charge."

Within a couple of days, three wagon loads of army provisions arrived for the impoverished Indians. When news of this reached the surprised agent, he hurried to find Bartlett.

"If the army wants to issue beef to Indians, I have some cattle to sell," he said. "I'll give you a good price."

"The hell you will!" roared Bartlett, whose words sent the agent scurrying away.

"That's another way white men make money off Indians," Sarah explained to the lieutenant. "That is one reason white men like to start Indian Wars."

Although Bartlett was in charge of soldiers after Captain Jerome went back to the Fort, Sarah had the job of issuing food to Indians, and she saw to it everyone had something to eat. However, the military stayed at the reservation waiting for further orders, and soon Sarah noticed Lieutenant Bartlett seemed to be at her heels everywhere she went.

"You know, I really should have come to Pyramid sooner," he told her one day.

She realized a compliment was implied and it pleased her. She liked the handsome, broad-shouldered, young lieutenant and his direct, honest manner in dealing with her and her people. He always seemed happy and laughed often. This pleased Sarah who was fond of a good joke and in less troubled times liked to sing and dance.

Before a week had passed, Bartlett received a message from the fort. He called Sarah and Natchez to talk to them about it. "The commanding officer wants to know if you can bring your people to McDermit where they can be fed and cared for," he told them. "He would like for your father, Chief Winnemucca, and Paiutes with him to come, too."

Sarah looked at Natchez, translating the lieutenant's words to be sure her brother understood. "It is all right," Natchez said, nodding his head thoughtfully.

"There's more," Bartlett went on. "He would like for you, princess, to be an interpreter at the fort. For this service, the government will pay you sixty dollars a month."

Sarah turned a frank, level gaze on the lieutenant. "We will do whatever you say. At least, we will try it. But I will have to explain it to my people."

"And your father—Chief Winnemucca?"

"I do not know if he will come. We'll have to wait and see how it works out," she replied.

But when Sarah told Paiutes of the offer, they turned startled faces toward her. "We do not trust white people," they said. "White people do not tell truth."

Again, Sarah explained to them about these soldiers from Fort McDermit. "They tell truth. They are *real soldiers,* not just white people. Because some white people are bad does not mean *real soldiers* are bad, too."

From then on, Paiutes always made a distinction between *white people* and *real soldiers.*

The task of moving tribes to Fort McDermit was not an easy one. First, Sarah went into detail, explaining carefully what she wanted the Indians to do. She knew that if they understood, and agreed to go, there would be no trouble at all.

"Our soldier-fathers tell the truth. They will give you food and blankets," she assured them, over and over again. At last, nearly five hundred Indians consented to the move.

In days past, the "moving-of-a-camp-time" was a merry occasion, with visiting back and forth, singing, races and games of chance. But now, their hearts heavy with thoughts of their dependent future, Indians only prayed to their good father in the spirit-world they would not get sick, but feel well on the trip.

In the early morning hours of July 1, 1867, Sarah and Natchez started to Fort McDermit with a courageous group of scantily-clad men, women and children.

58]

They were escorted by the soldiers. The migration was a slow-moving and pitiful procession. Some very old ones were in wagons provided by the army, some rode horseback and others trudged along on foot, all carrying their few possessions in baskets strapped to their backs.

"We'll have to stop often and rest," Sarah told the military.

The only member of this slow march who added any joviality to the ordeal was an old donkey the Indians loved too much to leave behind. They called him Wee-choo. He was a natural-born comedian whose antics were as welcome as the first tender shoots of cattails in the spring. For years, amusing tricks and ridiculous posturings of this animal had delighted old and young alike at every tribal race or feast.

With the Indians, Wee-choo was tame and gentle and would allow any of them, even small children, to climb on his back for a ride. However, no white man ever had this pleasure, although many of them had tried. No sooner would one manage to get astraddle the old donkey than he would find himself flying through the air.

On one occasion, a tall, thin white man who visited the reservation boasted *he* could ride Wee-choo. His legs were so long and skinny he made the Indians think of a grasshopper as he tried to get on Wee-choo's back. At last, he thought he had the animal in a proper position, and took a leap which carried him over the donkey's back and landed him in a sitting position on the ground, far beyond.

During this trip to Fort McDermit, children took turns riding their old pet, who was now bone-thin. Wee-choo seemed to know that he, too, would fare better with the soldiers than on the reservation.

They arrived at their destination in late afternoon of July 28, as the setting sun wrapped thin veils of lavender and dark blue around distant mountain tops. Sarah looked all around, scanning an area which stretched far away into the distance.

"This will be all right," she told Lieutenant Bartlett, who had been almost constantly by her side during the long trip. "There will be plenty of room here, and for my father and the ones with him, also, if we can persuade them to come."

Bartlett looked at her with admiring eyes. "I'm glad." His feelings for her were reflected in his face as he added, "I'm glad you're going to be near the fort, too, princess."

She looked away quickly, to hide her own feelings. "Whatever in the world is the matter with me?" she asked herself, for just the sound of his voice made her heart beat pleasantly faster.

When tents and blankets had been issued, and Sarah checked to make sure Indians were all right for the night, she went to her own room at one end of the main building. It was plain and simply furnished, but a welcome retreat for the chieftain's weary daughter. She lit a candle and set it on a small writing table by her bed, closed the door and slid a wooden bar across it. Then, she undressed and sank, exhausted, into her bed. It had been a long, hot, dusty trip, but they had made it safely and now her people would be cared for.

Sarah slept soundly, but was up early next morning slipping through the building's narrow corridor to the outside. She looked over a wide expanse of two thousand acres of open land which had been staked off for Indians. She heard murmurs of happy voices drifting through the clear, dry air while thin ribbons of smoke from campfires curled silently toward a cloudless sky.

She turned toward the fort to get a better look at it in the light of day. There were two more stone headquarters buildings, barracks, and a three-room infirmary. Beyond these were storehouses and stables. High on a pole anchored securely in the center of a courtyard, the Stars and Stripes fluttered gently in an early morning breeze. For once, Sarah had a deep feeling of gratitude for her country. Perhaps this flag would mean security and peace for her people now, as well as for the white race.

After breakfast, Sarah and Natchez were summoned to the commanding officer's quarters. "General Crook is rounding up all Indians not on reservations," he told them. "It's dangerous for Winnemucca to be out in the mountains with this going on. He's much too old, and he's likely to be killed. Do you think you can persuade him to come here?"

Natchez looked at the officer. "If you will give me your heart and your hand that you will live up to your promises, sir, I will go and find my father and try to get him to come."

"I will do everything I have said, Natchez, and I'll send a company of soldiers with you for protection."

"I do not want soldiers to go with me. Paiutes will think they are coming to fight. I will go alone. I can make the son's signal-fire as I go along so my father will know I am the one who is coming to see him." He hesitated, not liking to ask for favors. "There is only one thing, sir. Will you give me a piece of paper to tell white people I meet who I am, so they will not kill me. You know, sir, some white men like to kill Indians."

"Yes, I know," the commander replied unhappily. "Yes, I'll give you such a paper, but I cannot let you go by yourself. I'll send only five soldiers with you."

Very early next morning the six men left, riding north toward Oregon's Steens Mountain where Natchez and Sarah thought their father would be.

Before Natchez mounted, the commanding officer stepped forward, extending his hand. "My heart and my hand, Natchez," he repeated his promise.

Natchez nodded, his face solemn. "Do not let anything happen to my sister."

Sarah smiled at his concern. She touched the sheath-knife which always swung from her wide, beaded belt. "Do not worry about me, dear brother. Just bring our father back safely."

As she watched the horses disappear at a fast trot over a hill north of Fort McDermit, the Indian princess had a lost, lonesome, hollow feeling and was glad she had a great deal to do during the next few days and would not have time to worry.

She was in charge of issuing rations. She also acted as a guide to Indian families, who had fled other reservations, and got them settled near the fort for protection. These jobs were in addition to her official task of interpreter.

Every morning at five o'clock, Sarah handed out meat and freshly-baked bread to Indian women. Once a month she gave them coffee, rice, sugar, salt, pepper and beans. All clothing was of the type soldiers wore.

Lieutenant Hopkins was in charge of the commissary. He and Sarah became friends almost at once, and in his quiet, unassuming way, he helped her all he could, doing his best to take some of the load of responsibility from her shoulders.

The commanding officer gave Sarah an opportunity to talk with him anytime she had a problem or needed help in any way. On one occasion, she asked him, "Please, sir, will you give an order for settlers in the area not to go to Indian camps? Some of the white men treat our women shamefully."

At once, the officer had an order posted in conspicuous places on premises and outside boundaries of the fort. He never questioned Sarah's judgment in requests of this kind, and possibly saved himself a great deal of trouble by cooperating with her in matters which concerned the Paiutes.

Although Sarah had a room in one of the buildings, she mingled with Indians as much as she possibly could. It lifted her spirits to catch a faint whiff of tobacco mixed with the stronger fragrance of sage, for it reminded her of Council Tent days.

It made her heart glad to see Indian women bending over their cooking fires again, singing and visiting with one another. Now, they had the heart to mend baskets and shredded bark moccasins with bits of grasses and bushes found around the fort. When Sarah told them Natchez had gone to bring Chief Winnemucca, their faces brightened.

At last, one evening Sarah heard them coming. She looked into the distant autumn twilight, and saw a long caravan straggled out as far as she could see—men, women and children, on horseback and on foot, with her father and Natchez in the lead. On flying feet, she ran to meet them.

Just over the hill they stopped and Winnemucca dismounted. Calling his name over and over, breathless with joy, Sarah threw herself into her father's arms and he held her close.

"My child! My child! My child!" he said, over and over again.

Tears were running down Sarah's cheeks as she held her father at arm's length and looked at him. He was dusty and ragged and his face was thin and gaunt, but he still held himself proudly and the look of the Big Chief was still in his eyes.

"It is all right now, father," Sarah told him. "Now that you have come, everything will be all right."

The commanding officer came to meet Chief Winnemucca and wrung his hand warmly.

"Like for many moons, we come with peace in our hearts," Winnemucca said.

"It is a great honor, chief," the officer replied, smiling broadly.

With Lieutenant Hopkins' help, Sarah issued supplies to the newcomers and they soon set up camps. There were now nearly a thousand Indians at McDermit being cared for by American soldiers. They were happier than they had been for a long, long time.

"It is almost like the old days," Sarah remarked to her father.

"It is good. But we must do our part," Winnemucca replied. "We must help our soldier-fathers."

So, Indian men and boys cut pine and juniper for fence posts, gathered firewood and looked after cattle. With the officer's permission there were hunting and fishing excursions. Women and children went into the hills to dig roots, gather autumn seeds and pick wild berries. Back in camp, they dried meat, ground seeds into meal and cured animal skins for clothing. With food in their stomachs and proper shelter and apparel, Indians once again found the incentive to help themselves, and by late fall had stored up a good supply of provisions.

For the first time in many moons they held a celebration, with dancing, singing and games of chance. It had been a long time since they had felt like doing it. Now, once again, they had hope for the future.

» *7*

To liven up military life at Fort McDermit, every so
often soldiers would plan a dance. Congenial white
settlers who lived nearby were invited, especially those
who had daughters. Sarah, happy and confident with
high hopes of continued army supervision for the Paiutes,
entered into the spirit of these affairs and usually rode
out into the mountains with Lieutenant Bartlett for
greenery and flowers to decorate the large room in
which the dance was held.

She also prevailed upon one of her white friends
in Virginia City to donate an organ to the worthy cause,
for there was a captain who knew how to play it. Two
soldiers had fiddles and one could whistle very well.
And so they formed a band of sorts to furnish dance
music. The organ had seen better days and the pumping
of its pedal made a kind of wheezing sound, but it was
something like the beat of wire brushes on a drum and
added distinct rhythm to the music. The band sounded
good, even if its four members didn't always know the
same tunes. Nobody ever wanted them to stop and

constantly called for more.

Lieutenant Hopkins had established a reputation for making excellent fruit punch and it always fell to him to perform this task. He was very careful in blending fruits and berries, but to his great annoyance, Lieutenant Bartlett invariably came along and added some spirits. This potent punch became a joke throughout the area and eventually settlers called dances at the fort, a "Hopkins' Hop."

Sarah had learned to dance when she lived in Virginia City, and was always in demand as a partner. Bartlett tried to keep her for himself, but Sarah insisted on dancing with all who asked her, especially with Hopkins, for she liked him very much.

These two men who seemed to be the front runners in competition for Sarah's attention were as different as they could be. Hopkins did not have a flair for socializing nor the gallant charm of Bartlett, but the Indian princess found his sincere, homespun manner more than pleasing.

But as the days passed, it was Bartlett with whom she spent more and more time. He seemed to be conveniently around whenever Sarah needed help and he was always ready to escort her on a ride through the countryside to locate scattered bands of starving Indians and bring them to McDermit.

Soldiers gave the Paiutes needed protection and brought quick justice to white adventurers who took shots at Indians or rode horses through their camps. Bartlett was ready to back Sarah up whenever trouble arose, and she found herself leaning on his strength when there was a crisis of some sort. She rather liked the feeling of being a protected woman occasionally, although she was a tower of strength on which her Indian friends depended for support.

Sarah was very pleased with the way military supervision was working out for her people, although she hoped they could eventually be settled on land of their own. The commanding officer told her, however, the Department of Interior kept accusing the military of overstepping its bounds at McDermit.

"They keep insisting it is our job to furnish protection for settlers. They keep saying McDermit is an army fort, *not* an Indian reservation," he said.

"But Paiutes trust soldiers and will do anything for them, simply because you have always told them the truth. Can't the government see this?" Sarah asked almost angrily. "If Bureau officials want us on a reservation, then let the army be our agent."

The officer shook his head sadly. "They'll never do that, my dear. Don't you see, it's all politics? I'm afraid they're not too worried about what is best for your people."

By 1869, efforts and definite plans were being formulated by government officials to get all red men back on reservations and to close some of the army forts. Indians were strongly resisting this plan, mainly because of cheating agents who were in charge on many of the reservations.

This was brought back strongly to Sarah's mind when Chief Egan, who had stayed at Pyramid reservation with his tribe, came riding into Fort McDermit and asked Sarah if she would help him "talk" to the soldier-fathers.

Egan was one of the most respected of Paiute chiefs although he had been born a Umatilla. His father and mother were members of the Cayuse tribe which lived in a valley of the Umatilla River. When Egan was very small, his parents were killed. He had been found by a Paiute family who took him in and raised him as their own. He grew to be a very strong and handsome brave, famous among young Indian hunters, and married a sister of a Paiute chief. Later, he became the leader of a Paiute tribe and Sarah loved and respected him almost like a brother.

Army officers listened attentively to this handsome Indian who had all the features of his race, but never wore braids or ornaments. His hair, parted in the middle, hung short at his neck. Sarah interpreted as Egan told of the agent at Pyramid who made them give so much of what they raised to him, they could not provide for their families.

"When we ask agent why we have to give him so much, he tells us it is the order from Washington and we must obey." Egan's dark eyes clouded. "But I know that is not so. Someone is lying to us and we do not know what to do."

"Can you bring your tribe here?" an officer asked.

"They do not wish to leave their homeland. I have talked to them, but it is no use. And now, there is talk that more tribes are coming to live on the reservation. We do not have enough food for ones who are already there." He hesitated. "I thought soldier-fathers could tell me what to do."

"I'll have to think it through. If the Indians will not come here, there has to be another way."

Before Egan left, officers told him they would try to get help for Paiutes at Pyramid. Sarah walked with him to his horse.

"I am coming to Pyramid to see our people soon," she said. "Tell them to trust these soldier-fathers, for they always speak the truth."

About this time, Sarah began to actively involve herself in government affairs, trying to persuade the Indian Bureau to leave Paiutes under military control. With encouragement from officers at Fort McDermit, in April 1870 she sent a letter to Major Henry Douglas, superintendent of Indian Affairs for Nevada.

"Sir," she wrote, "I learn from the commanding officer at this post that you desire full information in regard to the Indians around this place with a view, if possible, of bettering their conditions by sending them back to Pyramid Reservation."

She went on to explain about her firsthand knowledge of living conditions on the Pyramid Reservation because she lived there for a time. She didn't go into detail about how they were treated, but stated simply if they had stayed, it would have been to starve. "If this is the kind of civilization awaiting us on the reserves, God grant we may never be compelled to go on one again."

She expressed hope that her people might someday have a permanent home where they could make their own living without encroachment by white settlers. She told him she realized Indians knew nothing about agriculture, but they were eager to learn and maintain themselves by their own labor if they could keep what they raised instead of having to turn it over to government agents.

Sarah finished her letter with a promise that if all of these things were done, ". . . I warrant the savage (as he is called today) will be a thrifty and law-abiding member of the community in time."

In a short while, Major Douglas came to Fort McDermit as a result of Sarah's letter. He talked to many Indians about their feelings on going back to reservations and found Sarah had told him the truth. Red men liked the army because soldiers kept their word, quite different from agents who were in charge of reservations.

Since her first letter stirred a little action on the part of the Bureau, Sarah decided to try a second one. In August of the same year, she wrote to Ely S. Parker, head of the Indian Bureau, protesting a transfer of her people from McDermit to Pyramid.

Sarah wrote this letter in much the same vein but in it she pointed out additional facts. Since the Central Pacific Railroad had gone through Pyramid Reservation and taken both land and timber reserves from them, the area was not large enough to provide a livelihood for Paiute Indians.
She wrote:

> Furthermore, at McDermit they have been accustomed to receiving their supplies regularly and have been allowed free access to all parts of the valley for purposes of hunting and fishing.

They do not want any change made now in their mode of life and will not go upon a reservation unless by force.

If the post be abandoned, and soldiers now stationed here be removed and if it be attempted to force them onto a reservation, their limits restricted, and their supplies curtailed by dishonest officials, they will become utterly demoralized and commence a series of depredations which will be very difficult to check and white settlers will have to flee.

I know more about the feelings and prejudices of these Indians than any other person connected with them; therefore, I hope this petition will be received with favor. Sir, I am the daughter of the chief of the Paiutes. I am living at Camp McDermit and have been in the employ of the United States government for three years as interpreter and guide.

This letter was not received favorably as the other one had been. In fact, it stirred up a commotion at the Indian Bureau. They resented Sarah's interference in their running of Indian affairs and implied she was presumptious and overbearing.

At the same time, her letter gave the secretary of Interior fresh impetus for accusing the army of trying to get control of Indians. So, Sarah found herself in the middle of a wrangle between the Department of Interior and the War Department. The army openly championed her purpose. Interior officials charged her with being in conspiracy with the soldiers.

Lieutenant Bartlett recognized this time of confusion, when Sarah needed broad shoulders to lean on, as being very opportune for pressing his own cause. He had long ago confessed his love to the beautiful Indian princess and had asked her many times to marry him. Although Sarah returned his affection, she realized there were many obstacles in the path of a happy union between them.

For one thing, there was a glaring fact they were not of the same color; that Bartlett, in fact, belonged to the whites, a race of people whose "ways" she utterly despised. Further, she was deeply involved in a long struggle to gain for Indians what was rightfully theirs.

Sarah did not doubt Bartlett's deep concern for the plight of Indians. He was often at her side when she rode to Pyramid, and she knew his heart was deeply touched by suffering and injustice he saw there.

"I sometimes wonder if it is worth the struggle to keep our race alive," she confided in him once as they rode slowly back to McDermit after such a visit. "It is only for future generations my people have the will to endure."

"Things usually work out, Sarah, if one keeps at them long enough," he'd try to cheer her. "Don't let yourself get too discouraged."

And then, because he knew she liked to ride like the wind, he'd challenge her to a race and they'd speed across wide stretches of sage-covered plains and along the spiraling mountain trails Sarah loved and knew so well. It was always a gamble who'd win because both were excellent riders and had fine horses.

These were times they liked best, when they were in the outdoors together. For although they loved to dance and made ideal partners, social affairs at the fort nearly always ended in an argument because Bartlett would invariably get drunk.

During this time, when the Department of Interior was attempting to get red men away from the army forts, members of the Indian Bureau had to swallow their pride and ask Sarah to act as interpreter at meetings between Nevada Indians and Bureau representatives to discuss the move to Pyramid Lake Reservation.

With Bartlett as escort, she rode to Oreano on the Humboldt, to the town of Austin in a steep Toiyabe Canyon and had several sessions with Indians who lived along the Walker River.

She thoroughly enjoyed these trips through a beautiful winter world, with the man she was learning to love at her side. It was perhaps this close contact with Bartlett through the winter which finally made Sarah throw aside her doubts concerning him and in February, 1871, answer yes.

The Paiute princess married her lieutenant in Salt Lake City, and when the newlyweds returned to Fort McDermit, they moved into housekeeping quarters. The only change which had been made during their brief absence was in the commissary. The gentle, smiling face of Lieutenant Hopkins was missing.

When Sarah asked about him, the commanding officer told her Hopkins applied for transfer and had gone East. Sarah wondered why he never mentioned he was planning such action. Perhaps some emergency in his family had caused him to make a quick decision. For whatever reason, she missed him and the many helpful things he did to make her work a little easier.

At first, Sarah was very happy in her married life, but as days slipped into weeks and weeks into months, the lieutenant began slipping, too. His desire for alcohol was a growing sickness and he began to drink at all hours of the day and night. The precious glamour of courtship and early-married days faded. Sarah was worried and full of concern when she had to be away. More and more often she returned to find Bartlett in a drunken stupor. When he sobered up, he was always sorry and full of promises to do better, but sometimes the very next day he would drink himself into unconsciousness again.

At last, the proud Indian princess had to face the reality that even though her husband of less than a year had many admirable qualities, he was a drunkard and their marriage had been doomed before it even started.

With her heart heavy as a stone in her breast, she began proceedings for divorce and Bartlett went back East. Sarah stayed on at Fort McDermit, plunging into her work with grim determination and concealing her heartbreak behind a deceptively stoical face.

» 8

From 1869, through eight years of the Ulysses S. Grant administration, drastic changes were made in the Department of Interior concerning Indians, with hopes of bettering the situation. By this time, Congress had passed a law declaring that no Indian nation or tribe would be recognized as an independent. The red man was not a citizen nor an alien, but a ward of the United States government. As such, the Department of Interior declared its main objective would be the education of the Indian so he could better help himself.

Previously, reservation officials had been selected by politicians, but President Grant suggested the choice should be left to missionary boards who would choose men of Christian character for these jobs. Grant also appointed a board of Indian Commissioners, composed of patriotic citizens who served without compensation, to work with the Interior Department in distribution of funds appropriated for Indians.

All of this sounded very impressive, but the new "Indian Policy" was unable to make any progress. The biggest stumbling block, as it had always been, continued to be the agents in charge of reservations. Indians who lived at army forts continued to fare very well, but conditions at Pyramid and other reserves were more wretched than ever.

Sarah, determined to put the heartbreak of her wrecked marriage behind her, threw herself into the fight with fresh vigor. On a visit to Pyramid Reservation, she saw that their setup for helping Indians was worse than nothing at all. She decided to talk to military officials about it at their headquarters in California.

With a letter of introduction from the commanding officer at Fort McDermit, Sarah boarded a train for San Francisco. She was able to make the trip by rail only because Central Pacific officials issued passes to Indian chiefs and their families. This gesture didn't lessen her resentment toward the railroad company for taking so much Paiute land, but she was appreciative of the interest shown by Leland Stanford, the railroad's president, when she learned it was through his insistence even this much was done.

When she reached her destination, Sarah appealed to both Brigadier General E.O.C. Ord and Major General J.M. Schofield, explaining her problem to them.

"The government is willing to provide all my people need," she told them. "But supplies never get past the agent. Even though Indians now have a few wagons and some farming tools, they still buy seed at the agent's store to plant their crops. Nobody shows them how to work land efficiently and after a slim harvest the government man takes the biggest part of the yield for himself. When my brother, Natchez, questioned the agent he was told the Big Father in Washington made these rules and if he did not abide by them he would have to leave the reservation."

In conclusion, she asked, "I leave it up to you, gentlemen. Do you think Indians are being treated fairly?"

These army men promised they would do what they could and were successful in getting some supplies to Indians at Pyramid that fall.

General Schofield suggested Sarah go to Virginia City and talk with United States Senator John P. Jones about this matter, which she did on her return to McDermit.

The senator seemed impressed with her story and promised to see what he could do. She never knew of his efforts, however, and reflected that a man who had a fortune at stake in the silver mines was probably much more interested in national monetary affairs than in the condition of a few tribes of Indians.

In 1873, work started on Malheur Reservation in southeastern Oregon. The Indian land was to cover an area of over two thousand square miles, with twelve thousand acres of tillable soil. Drained by three forks of the Malheur River, it stretched far in all directions, with windblown sageland, wooded hillsides, clear streams and broad fertile valleys. The nearest white settlement was outside its northern boundary at Canyon City and Camp Harney marked its western border. Sarah had high hopes that her people would be allowed to go there when they left McDermit, and it made her very happy when she was notified they could.

The Paiutes who lived in northern Nevada and Oregon, along with a few Idaho Bannocks, went to Malheur Reservation. Egan succeeded in moving his tribe there from Pyramid, and most of the Indians who had been camped at McDermit made Malheur their new home. Wee-choo, now plump as a "buckberry-in-the-ripe-time," made the trip with them. Sarah was disappointed when Chief Winnemucca decided not to take his band there, but went instead to camp with the soldiers at Fort Harney.

When the first Malheur agent appointed by the Missionary Board did not get along with Indians, Sarah's heart sank. She was afraid it was going to be the same old story all over again. But when he left in 1874, an Oregon pioneer, Samuel B. Parrish, took over the job. He was the best thing that ever happened to Indians

Oregon State Highway Department

Succor Creek wends its way through the rugged canyon it has cut through the centuries in the rock of the Owyhee Mountains in Oregon.

76]

of the area, even though he was selected only because there was no one else available at the moment.

Although Mr. Parrish was frank and honest in his dealings with everyone, he did not measure up to the Missionary Board's religious standards because he never gave money to a church nor attended its services. Frail of stature, but strong on moral ethics, this quiet, unassuming man hated religious hypocrisy, and lived his own uncluttered life by the Ten Commandments. He was the kind of leader Indians needed to adjust to reservation life.

When Sarah's work at Fort McDermit was finished, she rode to Montana to visit her sister, Elma, who had married a white man, John B. Smith, and lived near Bozeman. They had a happy reunion and it cheered Sarah to find the marriage was working out well.

After a short visit, Sarah went to Fort Harney to see her father and brother, Lee. She hoped to find employment there, but instead found a letter waiting from Mr. Parrish, offering her a job as interpreter at the new Malheur agency.

"I do not think I want the job," Sarah told her father. "I do not get along with agents."

"I think you should do it, my daughter," the old chief advised.

"Will you go with me if I do?" she asked.

After some thought he answered, "Yes, dear child, I will go, if that is what you want."

Sarah liked Mr. Parrish immediately. He gave her a room in a wooden agency building which had been erected on the west bank of the river's north fork and after she was settled, asked her if she would call the Indians together.

"Tell them to sit in a circle as is their custom when there are important things to discuss. This will make them feel more at ease."

As Indians took their places at this first meeting, Agent Parrish sat in their circle with them. As they talked, he smoked as they did and listened to what they had to say.

"You are my children," he told them kindly. "I am here to help you. I am not like the man who just left. I can't look up at the sky and pray for sugar and flour and potatoes to rain down as he did, but I will try to do my duty. I am here to show you how to work, and work we must."

Grunts of approval and sighs of deep thought went around the circle as Sarah translated words.

"The first things we must do are make a dam and dig a ditch," the agent went on. "This is to irrigate land so we can grow food for our families and for our horses and ponies. Some can dig a ditch, some can build a dam and some can go into the woods and cut rails to build fences."

"Yes, yes," they agreed, heads nodding.

"All that you raise will be your own to do with as you like. The reservation is all yours. The government has given it to you. There are some things we can raise this summer. We will plant potatoes and turnips and watermelons. We will not plant wheat because we have no mill to grind it, but we can raise oats and barley. When we get started, I will write to your White Father in Washington to send us a mill to grind our grain."

"Good. Very good," Indians said to one another.

"Before long, I will have four men here who can teach you trades. Some of you can learn to be carpenters and some blacksmiths. We must build a schoolhouse so your children can have an education. My wife will be the teacher."

When he had finished, Chief Winnemucca arose and spoke. "Let us work! Indians will work in fields! I will take Indians to dig ditch! Indians go to hills and cut rails! Indians build dam!"

And Indians did. They finished the ditch in six weeks. It measured ten feet across and two and a half miles in length.

"I must tell you, Sarah told Mr. Parrish, smiling broadly. "At Pyramid, they have been working on a ditch fourteen years and have only three miles of it done."

When the dam was completed and crops in their fields were beginning to grow, Mr. Parrish called for another Council. "It makes me very glad to see you work so willingly," he said to the Indians. "Your other agent told me you were lazy and would not work."

This statement sent them off into gales of laughter. "How could we work when he did not tell us what to do?"

"Since you have been so good to do as I asked," Mr. Parrish went on, "after the hay is cut, you can go hunting and get some buckskins. I know you will like that."

Winnemucca looked pleased. "Do you not think this is the best Father we ever had in our lives?" he asked his people.

"Yes," they all agreed. "We will do what he wants. He is a good Father—he talks truth."

All the way to their camps through a sage-scented wilderness, they kept repeating Chief Winnemucca's words, "He is the best Father we have ever had in our lives."

After Indians had harvested their crops, Mr. Parrish told them again that all they had grown belonged to them. Since he had two horses of his own, he said he would need some hay and grain but he would pay them for it. The Indians could scarcely believe their ears.

"I'll also pay each Indian a dollar a day when he works for me or any of my men. If you cut or pile wood, I'll pay you for it. If I send you to Canyon City on an errand for myself or any of my men you'll be paid for it." He looked around into approving faces. "Do you like this plan?"

"Truckee! Truckee!" they happily responded.

Soon, one morning before sunrise, Chief Winnemucca and all Indians who wanted to go hunting headed north. They believed that hunters who were in bed after sunrise would have bad luck. The Paiutes returned with buckskins and dried venison in plenty of time to dig potatoes and get them put away for winter.

By now, carpenters had the schoolhouse almost finished and part of government supplies had arrived. Sarah felt greatly encouraged and had the time of her life issuing red and white blankets to all Indians. Also, each woman got ten yards of calico, ten yards of flannel and ten yards of unbleached muslin. The boys and men received shirts, pants, hats and shoes.

It was a happy band of Indians who celebrated that night in a land where both moon and stars seem close to the earth. They danced around agency buildings and sang songs, made up as they went along, about their good Father Parrish. Sarah stood outside her small room, watching and listening, her heart full of happiness. And yet, intuition told her it was too good to last.

There were only two serious problems on the reservation that fall and winter. One occurred when some Columbia River Indians appeared and tried to get Paiutes to join them in a northward trek.

Chief Winnemucca told Mr. Parrish, "They are our enemies. They cheat us and always bring trouble. Make them go away."

This was all Agent Parrish needed to know. He applied a little diplomatic pressure on the unwelcome visitors and they soon left.

The other problem concerned Oytes, a Paiute chief who called himself a medicine man and refused to work. Ugly in appearance, but quick-witted and sly, he claimed supernatural powers and frightened other Indians by telling them of his dreams. He made the rounds of camps, relating such things as, "It is wrong to dig up the face of the earth. The earth is our Mother. We must live upon what grows of itself." Then, he would brag, "I can defeat all our enemies! I have the power to kill any of you! No bullet can hurt me!"

Finally, Egan went to Mr. Parrish and told him about Oytes. "He is wicked, but he has influence among some of our people. He will make them discontented. They will become idle and worthless."

"Thank you for telling me about it, Egan," Mr.

Parrish said. "I will take care of Oytes."

After a time the agent sent Sarah for this self-styled medicine man and asked her to summon other chiefs, also. When they came, Mr. Parrish took a loaded rifle in his hand and walked over to Oytes.

"I have heard you claim no bullet can hurt you. I have three hundred dollars in the bank. If you will stand up straight before me and let me fire a bullet from this gun directly at your heart, and if it passes through your body without harming you as you say, I will give you the money—all of it."

There was a long silence. Suddenly, Oytes turned to run but Egan blocked his path. "Aren't you going to let him do it?" the chief asked.

Poor Oytes was much too terrified to think of being boastful now. To Sarah, he said, "Tell him I am wicked, wicked. Beg the good agent not to kill me. I will work and never give any more trouble." And Oytes kept his word as long as Mr. Parrish remained at Malheur.

That spring, lessons started in the new schoolhouse with nearly four hundred eager children, young men and women as students. Mrs. Parrish, whom Paiutes called their 'White Lily Mother,' brought her own organ to the school and played an accompaniment while students sang. Windows were opened wide and warm spring winds carried melodies far across desert plains.

Mrs. Parrish was interested in all of the Indians, but one little girl, named Mattie, became very special to her. A niece of Chief Egan, Mattie had grown up in his home when her own father and mother had died. Her uncle and aunt were very kind to her, but the child's heart was won over by Mrs. Parrish. Although this little girl couldn't understand the white woman's language, she responded to her gentle manner. No white person had ever looked at her as pleasantly nor spoken so kindly.

Every day, the affectionate child picked wild flowers for her teacher and it made Mattie very happy when Mrs. Parrish put them in a vase on her desk for everyone to see. At last, she worked up enough courage to ask Sarah to tell Mrs. Parrish what was in her heart. "You are very dear to me," Mattie said. "You know I have no mother, so I have more love to give you than most of the children."

When Mattie grew up, she became the wife of Lee Winnemucca and a dearly beloved sister-in-law to Sarah.

When Mrs. Parrish noticed the devotion in Sarah's voice and manner when she was around Indian children, and saw their quick response to her, she asked the Indian princess if she would want to help with teaching. She was certain it could be arranged as soon as another interpreter was located.

Sarah was overjoyed and considered it a great opportunity to help educate Indian children growing up in a white man's world. She immediately began tutoring her cousin, Jerry Lang, in English so he could take over, freeing her to work in the reservation school.

9

Shortly after the school opened, General O.O. Howard and his seventeen-year-old daughter, Grace, accompanied by an aide, visited Malheur. The general, who had been in military command of the northwest territory for nearly a year, came to ask Indians' permission to build a post at Otis Valley, ten miles from the agency.

Paiutes gave their consent gladly. "You are our big soldier-father," they said. "We *want* you to come see us."

The guests, who had ridden through rough sagebrush country in a spring-wagon drawn by mules, were very tired and went to bed early. Sometime in the night they were awakened by loud noises coming from Indians' camps not too far away. The general who had experienced the sounds and sights of Apache war dances in preceding years, became alarmed and finally, around midnight, got up and went to find the agent to tell him of his uneasiness. Mr. Parrish assured him there was no cause for worry, but sent for Sarah and Egan.

Bureau of Ethnology, Washington, D.C.

Major General O.O. Howard, U.S. Army

Of Sarah Winnemucca's assistance to the United States Army, General O.O. Howard Commander of the Northwest Territory in the late 1800s alleged, *"She did our government great service, and if I could tell you but a tenth part of all she willingly did to help the white settlers and her own people to live peaceably together, I am sure you would think, as I do, that the name of Thocmetony should have a place beside the name of Pocahontas in the history of our country."*

Taken from *Famous Indian Chiefs I Have Known,* by General Oliver Otis Howard.

84]

"We were all so happy our big soldier-father had come to see us, and brought his daughter as well, we had to celebrate with a good feast and dance," the chief explained. "We are sorry to cause trouble."

"No trouble, no trouble at all," General Howard assured him. "Please, let the feasting and dancing go on." Then, he returned to his comfortable quarters and slept well the rest of the night.

In later years, he was asked about this experience at Malheur. The question was put to him, "What were you afraid of?"

General Howard replied, quite honestly, "My alarm was based simply on superstition that came from ignorance."

Next day before the general left, he talked with Sarah about Paiutes and the progress they were making at Malheur Reservation. "It makes me feel good to see you doing so nicely," he said. "I like to see all Indians getting along in this way. In time, you will be just like white folks."

Sarah did not wish to be rude, nor hurt the feelings of this good man whom she admired and respected, but she had to say, "Sir, it is good for my people to have advantages of white folks, but we do not want to be like white race. My people believe in telling the truth, and I would no more go to most white men for truth than I would go to the lowest valley for pine nuts."

General Howard smiled knowingly. He was impressed by her sincerity and her dedication to bettering the lives of Indians. After this visit, he referred to her as 'the sweet, sincere and spunky Paiute princess.'

General Howard had been gone only a few days when bad news came from Washington to Agent Parrish in the form of a letter. As soon as he read it, he called Sarah and told her of its contents.

"Settlers in Canyon City want the west end of Malheur Reservation, and some of them have been to Washington pulling political strings to get it." He held out a letter. "This is from President Grant. He wants to know what Indians think about it."

"I know what they will think!" Sarah cried in horror. "This is our land and we want to keep it!" She was remembering what had happened at Pyramid Lake Reservation when little by little, white people crowded in until there was no room left for Indians.

"I will get my father," she told the agent.

Chief Winnemucca came at once. "Dear Father Parrish, you must talk on paper for us to our great White Father in Washington and tell him we have no land to give to white people."

"I'll get a letter off this very day," Mr. Parrish promised. "They will not take your land from you as long as I am here."

Perhaps this statement was prophetic. Before many weeks had passed there was nothing more Mr. Parrish could do to help his Indian friends. Like a cruel and punishing blow, delivered for no reason that Indians could understand, word came from Washington that Samuel Parrish was to be replaced by another agent.

"Why?" Indians cried out, first in sadness and then in anger. "Why are they taking our good Father from us?"

This was a question for which there seemed to be no answer. Indians were prospering at Malheur, with more than a hundred acres covered with good crops. Although they had been awkward farming at first, Mr. Parrish had patiently showed them, over and over again, the right way to plow and harrow, furrow and plant, and they had made progress. The best part of it was that they had done the work themselves, and it was their own.

Indicative of prosperity at Malheur was the old donkey, Wee-choo. Although he had lost most of his teeth now from old age, Indian children ground grain between rocks and soaked it for him. Mr. Parrish gave them milk for him to drink, and the old donkey thrived on their loving care.

The same was true of little Indian ponies. Indian

children were kind to them and these animals showed very clearly their preference to the red race, and their dislike of white men. They didn't send their would-be riders flying through the air, as Wee-choo did, but they knew how to worry a white man to death.

In the first place, a pony that would let any Indian child catch him by the mane, lead him to a log, jump on, and ride as long as he pleased, would keep dodging a white man who was trying to get a hold on him. Then, if he did allow himself to be caught, he proceeded to keep twisting his head this way and that so it was all but impossible to get a bridle on him.

It was great fun for Indian youngsters to watch a white man trying to get a saddle on one of their ponies. With just a quick little shake of his body, the pony would twitch his blanket off to the ground, first on one side and then on the other, or make the saddle go backward or forward. However, once the aspiring rider got the saddle in place, he erroneously seemed to think the hardest part was over. He would get one foot up into the stirrup and then the pony would move just a little bit, making him hop with the other foot still on the ground, and then the little animal would move again, just enough to keep a man hopping after him on one foot. Indian children laughed and laughed as this performance went on time and time again while some white men didn't consider it to be such a good joke.

The days at Malheur had been filled with happy times—singing and dancing and feasting and working—and Indians did not want another Father to replace Agent Parrish.

The good man did his best to explain. "Your Big Father in Washington has written me the man who is coming to take my place is a Christian man, a better man than I. He lives in Canyon City and has a store there. His name is Rinehart."

Egan spoke up in a hard voice. "I know who he is. He is the one who sells firewater to Indians."

Winnemucca seemed stunned by the turn of events.

"My good Father, you shall not leave us. Say you will not go," he begged.

"It is not for me to say," Mr. Parrish replied. "I want to stay, but the government says I must go."

"We do not want anyone but you. I will go to see our soldier-fathers. They will help," the old chief kept on.

Mr. Parrish smiled. "They can do nothing against the government, chief, no matter how much they want to."

In spite of his words, Sarah, her father and Egan made a trip to Fort Harney to ask the army for help.

"I will do what I can," Colonel Green told them, and he did. He contacted General Howard and both did everything in their power to stop the change. However, orders were not reversed.

With a heavy heart, Mrs. Parrish had to close the school. Sarah was numb. Indians stood by and wept as the kind woman took leave of Malheur Reservation where she had done so much for Indians and had come to love and trust them, as they did her.

On an afternoon in early June, Agent Rinehart came galloping through the reservation on horseback. Tall and thin, with a drooping mustache and strange pale green eyes, he came to a halt in front of agency buildings, dismounted and impatiently brushed dust from his clothes. Sarah walked out of headquarters into the warm sunlight and looked this stranger over, sizing him up with calm dark eyes.

It seemed to make him nervous for his fingers fluttered toward his holstered gun. "You must be Sarah Winnemucca," he remarked in a drawling, nasal voice. "Where's Parrish?"

"He is out helping the farmers, sir. They are painting names on boards to put like a sign on their gardens and fields."

"On *whose* fields?" he inquired with a sarcastic smile.

"My people are farmers," Sarah answered politely,

missing his implication.

"Go get him!" he snapped, smile fading. "I'm Rinehart, and I'm here to take over."

Sarah started for her pony, but as she looked off into the distance she saw Mr. Parrish, still far away but riding toward them at a fast gait. She went back to Rinehart and told him, "He is coming." Then, she started back into the office.

"Indian!" Rinehart yelled angrily.

Sarah turned, frowning.

"Let's get one thing straight right now. When I say for you to do something, I expect you to do it, with no back talk. Understand?"

Sarah drew herself up proudly, her eyes flashing. "He is coming, sir," she repeated, pointing to a cloud of dust in the distance. Then, she walked into the building and closed the door behind her. "My poor people," she murmured aloud. "We are in for bad times now. I know it."

Through a window she saw Mr. Parrish arrive and shake hands with the newcomer. "My folks have already left, but I wanted to stay long enough to show you around the reservation," he explained.

"I've been over it before," Rinehart remarked impatiently. "I know what it's like. It's not important for me to see it again."

"Oh yes it is," Mr. Parrish insisted. "I want you to see what we've done because you wrote you intended to continue as I have started. The red men here are good Indians."

"I've never seen a good one in my life," Rinehart sneered. "An Indian's an Indian."

"You're wrong," Mr. Parrish said firmly, with a lift of his head. "For instance, I want you to meet my interpreter, Sarah Winnemucca." He motioned to Sarah. "She's—."

"We've met," Rinehart interrupted. "I've already got her straightened out about who's boss around here."

Sarah stepped out of the office, her back straight;

her eyes wide. "Did you need me, Mr. Parrish?" she asked, pointedly ignoring Rinehart.

"Will you ride around the reservation with us? Agent Rinehart wants to see projects we've started," Mr. Parrish said, his eyes telling her how sorry he was about everything.

"Yes, let's get started," Rinehart barked irritably and jumped astraddle his horse. He seemed to prefer taking no notice of Sarah's presence.

Mr. Parrish showed the new agent fences which Indians had built around their fields and gardens, an irrigation ditch they had dug and a dam they had built, the schoolhouse and a new road through the reservation to agency buildings that was still only partially finished.

"If you are fair with these Paiutes, you'll have no trouble," Mr. Parrish stressed over and over. "They are honest and willing to do anything reasonable that is asked of them. They have most of their crops in and it's been a favorable spring. We expect a good harvest this year."

They circled back to headquarters and Parrish took the new man to a storehouse to show him clothing and food supplies stacked neatly on shelves, lining all four sides of the room.

"These just came in," he explained, pointing to some stacks of clothing. "We haven't had time to issue them yet. Here are coats, pants, hats and shoes that really should be given to them right away so men won't have to wear blankets while they work."

Sarah noticed Rinehart was showing some real interest at the sight of all these goods stored on shelves. His strange eyes darted here and there, as though he were mentally adding up the worth of items.

"Sarah does the actual distributing of supplies and keeps a record just like she did when she was in charge at Fort McDermit," Parrish continued. "We issue food every day and clothing in the spring and fall."

Sarah had only a few minutes alone with her dear friend before he left. "I am afraid," she said simply.

"My heart aches for your people," Parrish replied, "but I have done everything I can. And now, I must leave you. It's all so wrong—so unfair to the Indians." He got on his horse slowly and headed north toward Canyon City.

Next day, the new agent's crew with their families swarmed in like a plague of crickets. They came in all guises—as a schoolteacher, a doctor, a blacksmith, a farmer and a clerk. Rinehart's wife and children were in the group also. To Sarah, they were the poorest and dirtiest looking white people she had ever seen, as ragged and undernourished as Indians at Pyramid Reservation. But within a few hours, they were all decked out in government clothing from the storehouse which had been sent for Paiutes.

As soon as the new agent had his own people fed, clothed and in their quarters, he sent for Sarah. "Tell the chiefs to come to me," he instructed her. "We need to come to an understanding." He kicked at a rock under his foot, not looking up. "Tell Old Winnemucca to come, too."

"My father has gone," Sarah told him. "And I do not know when he will return."

"Well and good," Rinehart muttered. "The fewer the better."

All of the chiefs came, silently, uneasily and stood in front of agency buildings on ground that Mr. Parrish had assured them was their own. Rinehart swaggered out of headquarters with a big show of self-confidence, yet kept a nervous hand on the gun at his side. He stood on steps, looking down at them.

"Sarah, tell them the Big Father in Washington sent me here," he ordered. "Tell them he sent me here to make all of you good people."

Indians hung their heads, murmuring among themselves, "He is not like our good Father Parrish."

"This land you're living on is government land," Rinehart continued loudly. "And you're working for the government. Let's get that straight right now. If you stay peaceful and continue to work, the government will pay you one dollar a day."

Sarah listened and interpreted, sick at heart. Malheur Reservation, off to such a good start was going to turn into nothing else but another Pyramid. After a long silence Sarah realized Rinehart was waiting for one of the chiefs to make some kind of reply to his remarks.

"Say something to him, Egan," she said.

"I do not have talk for one such as our new Father," Egan replied, his voice full of contempt.

"You must," Sarah prodded. "You will only make matters worse."

Egan stepped forward reluctantly. "Our Father, we do not understand your talk. We do not want you to fool with us. One man talk one thing and another talk something else. Our good Father who just left told us the land is ours and what we raise on it is ours also."

The agent, the good Christian man, flew into a rage as Sarah interpreted Egan's words. He started toward them, kicking childishly at rocks and pieces of wood on the ground. With one hand firmly on his pistol, he glared at the assembled chiefs. "I think you can understand this," he snarled. "If you don't like the way I do, you can leave! I don't care whether any of you stay or not."

"I do not want to leave," Egan replied softly. "I want to know who is telling truth."

"The man before me lied to you," Rinehart shouted.

Oytes touched Egan on the arm. "Do not say anything more," he advised, "It is of no use. Let us work first and see if he will pay."

With heavy hearts, Indians turned and started back to their camps. Furious because they had left before he dismissed them, Rinehart paced back and forth. As a parting shot, he yelled after them, "And when I tell you to do something, I want it done! And no damn' Indian is going to dictate to me!"

The Indians heard his angry voice but they did not know what he was saying. Sarah did not bother to translate these last words for she felt it no use to burden them more.

10

Next morning, Indian men, women and children went about their work as usual. Some cut rails or toiled in fields; some chopped firewood and hauled it in; still others smoothed dirt on the new road. Sarah continued her duties, issuing food and keeping her careful records.

The only visitor to the reservation that week was a man from Canyon City. Sarah did not know him nor his reason for coming. Rinehart sent her on an errand soon after he arrived and as she returned to headquarters sometime later, she saw his wagon heading back toward town.

On Saturday, which was payday for Indians, Sarah told Mr. Rinehart, "My people have come to get their week's money."

Without looking at her, he began to figure. "Let's see, men have worked six days—that's six dollars. Women have had sugar, flour, tea, coffee, beef—about four dollars worth of rations. That leaves them two dollars to buy anything they want out of the storehouse." He handed her a paper with some figures on it. "Here is a list of prices on clothing."

Sarah stared at him, aghast. "No, this is not right," she protested. "Supplies in the storehouse belong to my people. They are not yours to sell!"

Rinehart looked up quickly. "You just tell the Indians what I said. That's your job, nothing else."

Sadly, Sarah went to Egan first and repeated what this Agent had told her. With a few of his men, the young chief confronted Rinehart.

"Why do you fool us?" Egan asked. "We want our Father to speak truth, not tell us you will pay us money and then not do it. Our good Father Parrish told us things in storehouse are ours. If we have to buy clothes, give us our money and we can go to our soldier-fathers and buy better blankets than yours, for less money."

Rinehart answered, "If you want to buy your clothes somewhere else, I'll give you an order on a store in Canyon City where you can get nice things."

Egan's lip curled scornfully. "You think Indians are fools! I know clothes in store at Canyon City are from our own storehouse. I saw a man taking them away in his wagon." He looked over at Rinehart's wife and children who were standing nearby, taking it all in. "And besides, you and all your people are wearing things the White Father in Washington sent to Indians. We have not asked you to pay for them." With dignity, Egan turned to his men, "Let us go."

Rinehart flew into a rage, blood rushing to his face with anger. "If you don't like it, you can all leave!" he yelled. "No damn' Indian can talk to me like that! I won't allow it!"

The red men walked away slowly, not looking back. Almost beside himself, the agent turned, fixing his strange eyes on Sarah.

"You tell them—tell them—tell them what I said! Do you hear me?"

"Tell them yourself!" Sarah replied in a clear, firm voice and turned to follow her people to their camps.

The Indian princess tried to console them, but there

were no promises she could make. She knew in her heart the new agent was an evil man, under his facade of Christianity and feared events of this day were only a beginning.

During the night, one of Egan's men came to Sarah's door and tapped lightly. "Come talk," he said when she opened it just a crack. "Big trouble."

Once again, Sarah went to them and found many Indians gathered around their fires making muttering sounds of anger and fear. They asked her questions for which she had no answers. "How can we live through the cold time if our Father will not give us what we raise or earn? We will be hungry and miserable again as we were before."

All she could do was advise them to wait and see.

The next day was Sunday. Rinehart had made it very clear to Sarah he was never to be disturbed on his day of prayer. Neither could she issue rations, herself, because he had an only key to the storehouse.

"Indians can manage," he told her. "In fact, I don't think it's necessary to issue rations every day. Let 'em buy food if they insist on being paid for their work."

Sarah bit back sharp words which came to her lips. She was working for the government and felt she owed her allegiance to officials who were paying her, and still, she could not respect or even like this overbearing man who was her immediate superior. She wanted to keep her job as long as she could, but it was becoming harder every day to listen to his ranting outbursts against Indians and know he was scheming to cheat them out of what was rightfully theirs.

She stayed in her room most of that Sunday, pondering over the situation, trying to think of something she could do to help. Then, in the afternoon, decided to go for a ride to clear cobwebs from her brain.

Sarah had continued to work with Jerry Lang, giving him English lessons. All thoughts of getting to teach in the reservation school were gone now, but Sarah knew her cousin Jerry needed a job to support his family and interpreting was about all he could do since his eyesight was failing. She would ride out to his camp and give him another lesson.

As she arrived at Jerry's brush wickiup, she heard voices inside and recognized one as belonging to the despised Rinehart. "I'll find some way to get rid of her," he said. "And anyone who wants to be my friend can make a good living at that job, as long as you do what I say."

Sarah didn't even dismount, but rode away slowly. When she got back to headquarters, she was delighted to find her brother, Lee, with a group of Indians from her father's band, waiting to see her. They had come a long way and were very hungry.

"Mr. Rinehart will not issue any rations on Sunday," she told them. "But if you have some money, he probably will not consider it too much of a bother to sell you something."

As soon as the agent returned, Sarah told him the Paiutes wished to buy some food.

"All right, I'll sell them some," he replied. "Get my errand boy to open the storehouse for me."

The child he called his errand boy was a young Indian named Johnny who did little jobs around the agency from time to time. As soon as Sarah brought him, Rinehart tossed him a key and said, "Go get some beef from the storehouse."

The youngster started off on the run, but Rinehart had some second thought, got up and called out, "Hey, Johnny, come back!"

Evidently, the Indian boy didn't hear him because he kept on running. Rinehart, with sudden anger twisting his face, started after Johnny.

Sensing a thud of pounding footsteps behind him, Johnny glanced over his shoulder and saw Rinehart chasing him. He stopped and turned, puzzled. "What in hell do you want?" he asked as the agent came nearer.

"Don't you talk to me that way!" Rinehart yelled, reaching out to grab the boy by his hair. He shook him

th furiously. Frightened, Johnny wiggled
p, threw the key at him and ran away.

was out of his mind with rage. He ran
ne office to get his gun which he never carried
with him on the Sabbath. Sarah followed him, alarmed.

"I'm going to shoot him!" Rinehart snarled. "He's
not going to live another day. No Indian can talk to me
like that!"

Sarah could be quiet no longer. "No, you will not,"
she stated firmly. "You know Johnny does not understand those words. He was only repeating what he has
heard you say many, many times, and you will not touch
a hair of his head!"

Lee had followed his sister into the office. He spoke
in broken English, "We have come a long way to hear
good things from the spirit-man, and now you talk of
killing. You look up at the sky and talk to the spirit-
father three times a day, yet you would kill a boy who
meant no harm like you would kill a wild beast?"

These words seemed to bring the agent back to his
senses. He looked from Lee to Sarah and back again,
trying to get himself under control. Then, he said
gruffly, "I will take you to the storehouse."

As they walked along, Rinehart told Sarah, "I will
give these things to your brother and let you keep the
money for yourself."

Sarah could not believe her ears. Did the man think
she would cheat her own brother? Too, she remembered
what she had heard him say to Jerry Lang, and thought
he might be trying to fix it so she could be caught in
something dishonest. It angered her, and also made her
sad that this man had such a low opinion of the integrity
and moral standards of her people. He should believe
in them and trust them if he planned to help them at all.

"I am not the Big Father in Washington," she
replied. "I own nothing that is in the storehouse, so
why would I have the right to take money for it? If you
plan to cheat my people, please do not try to include me
in your schemes."

98]

Rinehart shrugged his shoulders, issued rations to Lee and his men and pocketed their money. After the Paiutes had eaten and rested for a short while, they went on their way.

That evening, Rinehart knocked on the door of Sarah's room. "Go and get Johnny," he said. "He must be taught a lesson for what he did today."

"No, I will not," she told him. "The child is innocent of any wrongdoing. He only repeated words he has heard you say."

"Very well. I'll send one of my own men after him, with these." He dangled a pair of handcuffs in front of Sarah.

"You wouldn't dare!" Then she looked into his eyes. "Yes, I believe you would," she said slowly. "I will go and get Johnny, but I will not allow you to hurt him."

The little boy was terrified when Sarah told him he had to go to headquarters to speak with the agent. "I will not let him harm you, I promise," she said.

As they walked to the door, Rinehart made a grab for the youngster, catching him by his shoulders and shaking him roughly. "I'm going to kill you!" he muttered, like one demented.

Sarah stepped forward quickly, her hand on a knife which always hung at her side. "Turn him loose!" she ordered. "You would not dare harm him!"

Rinehart cringed. "All right! All right! I'll just lock him up for tonight to teach him proper respect, and then let him go in the morning."

"If that is all you will do. If you are speaking the truth, I will explain it to him. He can understand that kind of punishment."

Rinehart promised over and over again, and in this instance, he kept his word. The results were not so painless the next time he lost his temper with a child. It was a tragedy which added to the burden Sarah was already carrying in her heart.

One evening, as the sun was getting low, she sat in her doorway taking in the pleasant vista of far-stretching land reflected by blues and pinks and orange-reds of the western sky. Suddenly, she heard a loud, pitiful cry of a child.

Looking around quickly, she saw Agent Rinehart throw a little round-faced boy to the ground and kick him on the side of the head with his pointed boot. The child rolled over, scrambled to his feet and ran away. Sarah sat, frozen with horror, unable to move. Rinehart saw her watching and came over to her.

"Now, listen, Sarah," he began to explain uneasily. "That little devil laughed at me. I was telling him to go get Jerry, and he laughed. I won't have any Indian kid laughing at me. I'll beat the life out of him."

Sarah managed to get to her feet to confront the half-crazy man. "Mr. Rinehart, that little boy was not making fun of you. He cannot understand one word of English and he thought you were saying something nice to him. Indian children always laugh when they are pleased. I do not know what to say to you, but this kind of thing cannot go on much longer." She went into her room, and closed the door.

In the night, one of the Paiutes came for her. The little boy's ear was swollen badly and his head was purplish-black. He could not speak. The Indian princess went to the man who had come to the reservation with Rinehart as a doctor, but he was in a drunken stupor. Heartsick and afraid, she administered to the child as best she could, but in the early morning hours, he died.

As a mournful wailing for the boy began, Sarah strode angrily to the agent's quarters and rapped on his door. He opened it, clad in his dressing gown and looked at her through sleepy eyes. "What in hell do you want, Sarah?" he grumbled.

"Just to tell you the little boy you kicked in the head, is dead. The white doctor was too drunk to help him and we didn't have the knowledge."

"Well, I'm sorry to hear that, of course," he said, avoiding her eyes. "But you people have to learn—."

"To learn what?" she asked. "That we must bow

and cringe and do everything you say or you will put handcuffs on our children or kick them in the head and kill them? Is that what we have to learn?"

"That's enough, Indian," he snarled, beginning to lose his temper. He stepped back and put his hand over a gun on his desk. This seemed to give him courage to continue. "From somewhere, you've got the notion you're some kind of privileged character around here. Well, to me, you're just a dirty, lying Indian like all the rest, and you can be replaced. Easy!"

"There is no use to talk to you," Sarah replied sadly. "You feel no more pain about causing the death of an Indian boy than if you had kicked a rock out of your path. I do not know what is to become of my people." She turned and left.

When fields were ready to harvest, Egan and Oytes came to have a talk with the agent about their grain. "We want to make sure it is ours, to do with as we please. This is what our good Father Parrish told us."

"If Parrish told you that, he lied!" Rinehart said. "Nothing here is yours. It all belongs to the government."

Sarah spoke up. "Mr. Parrish showed me a letter in which you said you would go on with us in the way he started, by giving us what we have raised. I told my people this is the way it would be. If you do not do it, they will never believe me again. They will think I tell lies like white men."

"Then, you might have to be replaced, eh, Sarah?" Rinehart smirked.

Egan stepped forward. "Sarah, I want you to tell this man everything I say." Then, he began, "Is it your job to try to run us off the reservation? Is that what the government wants you to do, so you can have our land? Is that why you cheat us and kill our children and carry a gun to kill us if we do not please you?"

Egan swallowed hard, and Sarah was aware of how difficult it was for a gentle, peace-loving man like this good chief to say such things to another. Still, he went on. "We want to know how the government came by this land. Is the White Father in Washington our spirit-father, or perhaps even mightier than the spirit-father? What have we done that he wishes to take from us all that he has given? Why does he let his white children come and take all our mountains, and all our valleys, and all our rivers? And now, that we have a little place of our own, that he gave us without our asking for it, he sends you to tell us to go away."

Egan pointed far away in the distance. "Do you see that high mountain over there? On it, there is nothing, only some rocks. Is that where the Big Father would like my people to go? Even though we scattered our seed there, it would not grow on the stony ground. Even so, if we should go there, I know your people would come and say, 'Go away, Indian. I want these rocks to build me a beautiful home!' "

Rinehart shifted back and forth on his feet, but kept his eyes lowered. He could not look the Indian in the face.

"Another thing," Egan continued. "you know we have no money and no way to get it. I have had only two dollars since you came which I gave you for a pair of pants. My son-in-law did the same." Egan took a step forward and Rinehart backed off. "That is all the money you will ever get from me. Tomorrow, I am going to tell the soldier-fathers what you are doing. They will tell me if it is right. They tell truth."

"Well, just go ahead," Rinehart sputtered. "Why don't all of you go and live with the soldiers? I have to do what the government says, and if you don't like it, leave!"

"It is no use trying to talk to him," Egan told Sarah. "He does not care what happens to Indians."

"I am afraid you are right, my dear friend," Sarah agreed. "He is a cruel, evil man and wants to get rid of any of us who question anything he does."

That night, Jerry Lang came to see Sarah. "What is the matter with you?" he asked. "What do you care whether Rinehart gives the others anything or not as long as we get our share? Our people really do not care for us. Let them go wherever they like."

Sarah looked at him, disgust written plainly on her face. "I am ashamed of you, Jerry. Those are not your words; our agent put them into your mouth. If you want to see your own people starve, that is your business, but I am here to work for them and help them as much as I can. I'll stand by them and talk for them as long as I live." Sarah stopped to catch her breath, and then finished. "If you are going to be like the white people, my cousin, do not ever bother me again."

Jerry said no more and departed.

The next day, Sarah went with Egan to Camp Harney to talk to the commanding officer there about their troubles. The officer advised Sarah to write a letter to Washington and have all chiefs sign it. He promised her he would write, also. "Surely they cannot ignore conditions such as these," he said.

Sarah wrote a letter and then took it around for all the chiefs and sub-chiefs of the Paiutes to sign. The commanding officer was right. The men in Washington did not ignore her communication. She received an answer right away, informing her that her services were no longer required.

This came as no great surprise to the Indian princess. She had been expecting it ever since she decided to tell Rinehart what she thought about things, instead of keeping quiet.

The agent could scarcely conceal his delight as Sarah packed her few belongings and moved out of the small room. She camped with her people for three weeks until she could find a place to go.

As she walked past headquarters one day, she saw Rinehart knock an old Indian man to the ground with a big stick and begin to beat him. She ran to them as fast as she could and caught the agent's upraised arm. "Stop it!" she cried. "What did he do?"

Rinehart shook her off roughly. "I don't have to tell you anything! And get out of here. An Indian needs to be beaten when he's lazy."

The old man got to his feet slowly. "I was trying," he said to Sarah. "I was going to do an errand for his woman, and was too long in putting on my moccasins.. I—."

"Lazy, good-for-nothing!" Rinehart growled, raising the stick to strike again. The old Indian caught it, and wrestled it from his grasp. The agent, face livid with anger, went for his gun.

At the same time, Sarah drew her knife and held it steady. "Do not you dare!" she ordered.

With a shaking hand, Rinehart returned his pistol to its holster. His eyes flicked from Sarah to the knife she still held. "I believe you really would kill me," he quavered.

"I am an Indian woman," Sarah replied grimly. "If you hurt him any more, you will find out!"

She stood, motionless, until the agent backed away.

11

When Sarah left the reservation, she went north to live with a white family who had settled on the John Day River. Paiutes wept to see her go, and little children to whom she had taught English words and meanings at every opportunity, stood with bowed heads. She worked very hard to make herself useful to the family who had employed her, but her heart was with Indians. She was determined to find a way to help them.

The first direct news she had from Malheur was in the early spring of 1878 when three braves came riding over snowy summits in search of her. They had been sent by Egan to ask her help. The men were thin, haggard and hungry.

Sarah greeted them joyfully, although stricken by their appearance. "Come in, and I will give you something to eat," she told them. "And then we will talk. You are as lean as the "jackrabbit-thin-with-the-dry-time.""

"It has been long since we ate," they admitted.

Sarah brought them meat and bread. They hunched

over the food, wolfing it down and not saying another word until it was all gone. "Good," they then said, nodding their heads.

The news they brought was very distressing. Rinehart had stopped issuing food now and any Indian who got supplies sent by the government had to buy them. "Most of it he sends to store in Canyon City to sell," they told her.

Sarah looked at the men, angry and distraught.

"Paiutes are dying of starvation," they went on. "Our animals have disappeared. Even Wee-choo is gone, and when we ask the agent where our ponies are, he calls us the bad white-man words."

"How can such things be allowed to happen?" Sarah asked. "Indians can make no money without their horses, and without money they can buy no food or clothing."

"But that is not all," the men went on. "Bannocks have come to Malheur and are riding the circle of encampments of Paiutes making words of war against the whites."

"Where is my father?" Sarah asked.

"Chief Winnemucca is at Malheur, trying to keep the peace, but his talk is lost in big noise all around. Bannocks keep coming from Fort Hall wanting Paiutes to join them in war."

The Bannocks were another tribe who suffered under unfair treatment. From very early times, they had wandered over western Wyoming, below the Salmon River in Idaho, and all along the Snake River from southern Montana into eastern Oregon. The main food of these Indians was the camas root and their *Big Camas Prairie,* in Idaho, was the principle source of this plant. In 1869, when the government set aside Fort Hall Reservation for them, they were told it would include their sacred camas ground.

It happened, however, that a federal clerk, in recording boundaries of the tribal lands, wrote "Kansas" Prairie, instead of "Camas" Prairie, and nobody bother-

106]

ed to correct the error. Whether this was just another political expedient for outwitting Indians or one of the many bureaucratic blunders, was never known. The outcome of the clerk's carelessness was that white settlers were allowed to move onto Big Camas Prairie.

Sarah knew of all this, but asked, "Has something new happened at Fort Hall to make Bannocks go on the warpath?"

"They are starving, as we are. The only difference is that our agent sells Indian supplies locally while the one at Fort Hall ships provisions to his relatives in the East."

"It is not fair!" Sarah blurted out. "There has to be something we can do!"

"That is why we came," the Indians said. "Our people sent us to ask if you will go to talk to our soldier-fathers or to the great White Father in Washington."

"I have no money to go to Washington," Sarah said, with a sigh. "And I am afraid if I talk to the soldiers, it will make matters even worse. Remember, the reason I was sent away from Malheur was because I reported Rinehart to the army. I will think of something, though," she assured them. "I must! The Paiutes must not go on the warpath."

With a grievous heart, she bid the three Indians goodbye and watched them until they were out of sight. She racked her brain to think of something she could do, but felt her influence was at such a low ebb right then, nothing she said or did would make the slightest difference to anyone.

In less than a month, the three Paiutes were back, and this time, they were desperate.

"Most Paiutes have been driven away," they reported. "They are camped along river, trying to live off the few fish they can catch. There are many Bannocks there, too, and all they can talk about is war against the whites. Egan is holding out for peace, but his men are leaving him and going to Oytes who is in favor of war. Please, dear *Thocmetony,* go to see our great White Father in Washington. Surely, he will help us."

Sarah made up her mind quickly. "Yes, I will do it," she said. "I will drive my wagon to the reservation in five days, and meet you at Egan's camp."

Joy flooded weary eyes of the Paiute braves. They galloped off with new hope in their hearts and the happy news for their people that Sarah was coming to help.

In the dark of the fifth night, Sarah met with Malheur Indians and told them she would go to Washington. For expense money, she planned to sell her wagon along the way and journey on horseback, if necessary.

"I must go as fast as I can," she told them. "We do not want our Indian brothers to go on the warpath against whites. That will not solve anything."

She didn't tarry after the meeting, but headed southeast that night. Before she reached old Fort Lyon, which was then a station on the stage line to Boise, she met a Paiute scout on her third day out.

"Bannocks are on the warpath," he told her. "They are killing every white they can find, and many Indians, too, who will not join them. They killed a stage driver and got guns he was taking to soldiers."

"When did the fighting start?" Sarah asked.

"Only one day past. A young girl, sister of one of Bannock Jack's band, went to Camas Prairie trying to find some roots to dig. Two white men saw her there and did terrible things—just a child. The girl's brother and another brave went after the two men and killed them."

"And so the chief was told he had to give two Indian braves to pay for the dead men," Sarah said dejectedly. "It is an old story, one that has been repeated many, many times."

"Yes, white settlers told the chief that all his people would be shot if he did not obey. But before the chief could meet their demands, whites stole all of the tribe's ponies and guns and left them helpless."

"I guess the whites just went too far this time,"

Sarah commented. "There is a limit, even to patience of the Indian."

"One brave managed to slip away. He ran to tell the other tribes what had happened to Bannock Jack's men. They went on the warpath and now no one is safe. You must go no further than Stone House. White people have come there to hide, and soldier-fathers are guarding it."

Alarmed at this news, Sarah asked the scout, "Have my people joined the Bannocks?"

"Not all. Some, with Oytes for their leader were among the first to fight, and since so many of Egan's men had already deserted him and left Malheur, he finally agreed to be their War-Chief and has joined the Bannocks in their fight."

"Oh, no," Sarah breathed with a sinking heart. "And my father?"

"I am sorry to have to tell you this, but Chief Winnemucca and his tribe have been forced to travel with the hostiles, against their will. I do not know where they have been taken."

"Are my brothers with him? Or did they go with Egan?"

"I only know about Natchez, and I cannot tell you for sure about him. He went to warn three white ranchers on the river that Bannocks were coming to kill them. When the hostiles came, he helped whites to get away, but his own horse stumbled and fell. It could not get up. Natchez yelled at the men he thought were his friends to wait and let him jump on behind one of them, but they would not. They left him to shift for himself against the Bannocks. Only the good spirit-father saved him. He hid in the thick brush and was able to slip away that night. I talked with him a few hours later, but I do not know where he is now."

"I thank you for what you have told me," Sarah said to this scout, and then hurried on down the trail to Stone House where a large number of citizens had fortified themselves in the three-room building. As soon as she drove up, soldiers with guns ready to use rushed out to gather around her wagon.

"Who are you?" they asked, betraying they were newcomers to the West by not recognizing the Paiute princess.

"I am Sarah Winnemucca, on my way to Elko, Nevada," she told them.

"You wait right here until I notify the officer in charge," said a pale-faced young guard, and he hurried into the building. Almost at once, a portly man in an officer's uniform came out and walked over to Sarah. He extended his hand. "Welcome, princess," he said, giving her a firm handshake. "I am Captain Hill, and I must tell you not to go any farther. The Bannocks would like nothing better now than to kill the daughter of Chief Winnemucca."

He helped Sarah alight from her wagon and they walked toward the building together. "I have heard many good things about you from General Howard."

Thank you," she replied. "General Howard is a good friend." Then, looking at him anxiously, "Do you have any news of my father?"

"He and his tribe have been taken prisoner by the Bannocks, and we do not know their whereabouts. Communications from McDermit and Harney have been cut off."

"Then you do not think this may be just a small skirmish, soon over?" Sarah asked hopefully.

"No, I'm afraid not. What happened to Bannock Jack's tribe merely set off plans that have been in Chief Buffalo Horn's mind for some time. I believe he had already made the decision to fight for Big Camas Prairie, no matter what the cost."

Sarah could imagine the pain in Bannock Chief Buffalo Horn's heart each time he looked across the once-beautiful valley which extended north to the Sawtooth mountains, and saw ranchers' camps spread out all over the prairie. She could imagine how he felt as nearly three thousand cattle trampled and ate the

110]

slim grassy leaves and lovely purple blossoms of the camas plant which furnished most of the food for his people. And even worse must have been the sight of hogs, rooting out bulbs of the plants with their long snouts and growing fat on them, as his people grew more and more thin and haggard. With deep hurt already in his heart and no relief in sight for his tribe's hunger, it was little wonder to Sarah that Bannock's chief took the path to war.

She heard in later years that her views had been shared by General Crook who had inspected Fort Hall Reservation just the year before this uprising. He expressed sympathetic understanding for the final acts of hostility. "Our Indian policy has resolved itself into a question of warpath or starvation," he had reported. "Being merely human, many of them will always choose the former alternative, where death shall at least be glorious."

Sarah spent a miserable day and night at Stone House. The soldiers, most of them very young and new to the territory, stared at her as if she were some kind of harmful beast. "We'd better put a guard on her wagon," she heard one of them say.

"Yeah, and the captain had better take that knife away from her, too, if he's smart," put in another. "I'll bet she really knows how to use it."

White settlers who had gathered there for protection were suspicious of her, too. They eyed her continuously and some of them made derogatory remarks about Indians for her to overhear. At every turn, she looked into tense, nervous faces, lined with fright of the red race. All of this, combined with her own worry about the safety of her father and brothers, kept Sarah on edge.

Finally, she went to the captain and told him. "I cannot for the life of me stand any more of this. I am not a savage, ready to murder anyone, and neither are my people. I am fearful for the safety of my loved ones as they are for theirs. Is there nowhere I could go to get away from their hatred and suspicion until it is safe for me to move on?"

"I am sorry, princess," the Captain apologized. "These people are hysterical with fright and they imagine things." He laughed as if it were a joke. "Some of them think you are taking ammunition to the Bannocks in your wagon."

Sarah did not think this funny. "I have never heard of such a thing!" she exclaimed. "I do not want my people to go on warpath! Tell them to go and look in my wagon. If they find anything more than a knife and a fork and a pair of scissors, I will give them my head to use for a ball!"

"Now, Sarah, you know I believe you," he protested. "I have told them over and over who you are and what you have done to help Indians and the whites reach an understanding. I certainly would not dream of searching your wagon."

Sarah suspected, however, the young and green soldiers had already given it a very thorough going-over.

Next morning, the army's Captain Bernard and his company came by Stone House on their way to Sheep Ranch where they were going to set up headquarters near Boise City. With the military were white volunteers and Indian scouts, one of them being Pi-Ute Joe, an acquaintance of Sarah's. They brought news of the death of Bannock Chief Buffalo Horn. Pi-Ute Joe had killed him, and he told Sarah about it.

"I went to South Mountain with citizen scouts, and we stumbled onto Buffalo Horn's camp. I was in front, but when I looked back, I saw citizen scouts running away and leaving me to face the Bannocks all alone. I saw I could not get away from these hostiles that were all around me. I jumped off, and put my horse between me and them, and laid my gun over the saddle and fired at an Indian who came galloping up, ahead of all the rest. It was Chief Buffalo Horn. He fell from his horse, and his men turned and ran away fast when they saw their chief was dead. That was all that saved me. I'll tell you, those citizen scouts were surprised when they saw me again. They left me to be killed by Bannocks. From now on, I go only with soldier-fathers."

Captain Bernard was glad to see Sarah. They had known each other since her days at Fort McDermit.

"What luck to find you!" he said, clasping her hand in a friendly grip. "We just left General Howard. He told me to try to find you and ask for your help in corralling the Bannocks."

Knowing the futility of a trip to Washington at this time, she told him truthfully "My heart beats with the Indians, but I know that war will only destroy our race. My people are in danger. I do not know where my father and brothers are, and I fear for them. But if I can be of any service to the army, I will do all I can to stop the bloodshed. I will stay with you until the war is over."

"Good!" Captain Bernard said heartily. "I'll send a runner with news to the general." With a firm hand he gripped her shoulder for a moment. "And, as for your feelings about the Indians' cause, princess, my heart beats in the same way as yours."

Sarah left Stone House on horseback the next morning with Captain Bernard and his command. A soldier drove her wagon which she donated to the army to use during the rest of the war. They waited at Sheep Ranch for a reply from General Howard, and by evening, a scout had returned with his message.

"Send Sarah with two or three friendly Indians straight to her people. Have her father send a few of his best men to you. Take Winnemucca and the others to McDermit. I will see they are properly fed and protected. Promise Sarah a reward if she succeeds, and give her my best regards."

None of the citizen scouts would volunteer to go with her, and even Indian scouts, when informed of General Howard's orders for Sarah, cried, "We will do anything for our soldier-fathers but that. We will go anywhere except to the hostile Bannocks. You do not know the danger. They will kill anyone who gets in their way."

Sarah returned to the captain with a determined look on her face. "No one will go with me," she told him. "But I will go alone."

"You can't mean that, Sarah!" Captain Bernard protested.

"Oh, but I do! If you will give me a horse to ride, I will be on my way."

Captain Bernard shook his head. "I don't think General Howard will allow it. It's too risky. Your life will be at stake."

"I want to find my father and my brothers," she insisted. "I am not afraid to go alone."

As they were talking, two braves of Sarah's tribe, known simply as Paiute George and Paiute John, came padding into the room on their soft-soled moccasins. "We have been told Thocmetony is going to go alone into danger," Paiute George said. "I cannot let her do that. I will go with her."

"I will go, also," Paiute John announced.

"Good!" Captain Bernard exclaimed, all smiles. "You will be paid well."

"That is unimportant," Sarah replied. "But will you give me a letter to take so if our horses give out and we have to stop at a ranch to get another, white men will not shoot us on sight?"

"Of course, of course."

Captain Bernard sat down at once and wrote:

To all good citizens in the country: Sarah Winnemucca, with two of her people, goes with a dispatch to her father. If her horses should give out help her all you can and oblige.

Captain Bernard.

» 12

In the first daybreak hours of early June, 1878, Sarah, with two Paiute braves, set out from Sheep Ranch to find hostile Bannocks and to look for her father. They carried only a few supplies in packs and some blankets under their saddles. Sarah dropped in her pocket cakes of warpaint which scouts had picked up in enemy territory. "We might need these," she said.

They headed for Oregon's Steens Mountain , a distance of over a hundred miles through some of the wildest, loneliest, roughest wooded country in the West. Sarah wasn't worried; she had the know-how for such a trek. From the cradle, she had learned the Paiute way of life which would guide her through unchartered wilderness. She could find directions by positions of the sun and stars, and knew which native plants would furnish nourishment to supplement their food supply. Her heritage had given her the gifts of strength and courage and endurance to face dangers of this journey. She was an Indian woman.

At Owyhee River Crossing, fifteen miles from Sheep

The Owyhee River cuts its tortuous route through the rocky plateau area of southeastern Oregon.

Ranch where patrol headquarters had been set up for the area, Sarah found all of the white men stationed there, fast asleep.

"This is what citizen scouts are good for," she told her men. "The government pays them twenty-five dollars a day and this is how they perform their duties. They go off a little way from troops and lie down and rest, and then come back and report there are Indians close by, just to make soldiers think they are on the job."

She couldn't pass by without awakening them. "Is this the way you keep watch for hostiles?" she called out, her voice loud and cross.

Citizen scouts awoke with a start and a mad scramble for their guns. "Who are you?" they chorused, wide-eyed and scared.

"Fortunately for you, I am Sarah Winnemucca with two of my people, going to locate the Bannocks' camp. If we had been hostile Indians, we could have killed every one of you, very easily."

About a mile beyond the Crossing, the trio struck a trail of warring Indians and followed it down the river, finding signs of sadness and death all along the way. They came to an area where there had been weeping, cutting of hair, tearing of clothing and breaking up of beads, all in grief and mourning for loved ones.

After a time they left the river and headed toward Barren Valley, noticing a leather whip lying in the dust where the stage driver had been killed and his load of guns stolen.

The three Indians rode hard all day and far into the night, taking no time for rest until, in the darkness, their horses could not keep a sure footing on the rough, rocky ground.

"We must stop. Our horses will fall over and kill us and then the Bannocks will not have the pleasure," Sarah informed her companions.

They made camp, ate hard rolls and rested until dawn, then started across Barren Valley at a good clip.

The Steens Mountain Range rises abruptly from the dry
plateau floor of southeastern Oregon, overshadowing the
rippled surface of Mann Lake.

Steens Mountain attains a height of 5000 feet above the far-
flung expanses of Alvord Valley which, itself, is 4000 feet
above sea level.

Soon, the party came to a ranch where a settler's house was nothing but a pile of smoking ashes. Undoubtedly, Bannocks were not far away yet they stopped for a moment to look around. With so many fresh pony tracks the two men were uneasy and urged Sarah to go on without delay.

She faced her two friends with a solemn look. "There is no use for us to be afraid," she told them. "We have come to find the Bannocks, and find them we must. If they kill us, then we must die, and that is all there is to it."

Riding on, studying the lay of the land, they decided it wise to follow a faint trail to Steens Mountain and continued on as fast as their horses could travel, toward Juniper Lake.

In the late afternoon, Sarah spotted a man in the distance running up the mountain slope, and as they approached he disappeared into thick underbrush.

She gave a cry of joy. "Unless my eyes are failing me, that is my brother, Lee." Riding closer, she gave a low whistle and then listened. There was no reply. Sarah whistled again, a certain special sound with which she had always announced her arrival to the family. This time, there was an answer, like an echo, drifting back to them through the high country's thin air. "I knew it was Lee!" she cried happily.

Her brother emerged from the brush and came running downhill. Sarah jumped off her horse and hurried to meet him. They threw their arms about each other.

"Oh, my dear sister, you have come to save us!" Lee cried. "We are prisoners of the Bannocks and cannot get away."

"Where is our father?"

"Over that mountain." He gestured in a direction which had no trail.

"I must go to him."

"I am afraid for you. You will be killed!"

"I am not afraid. I have a message for him from

General Howard. I have to help him and our people, no matter what happens. That is why I came, and our two friends came with me."

"Then unbraid your hair, quick, so you will look like one of them."

"I can do more than that." She reached into her pocket and brought out the cakes of warpaint. Then, she rubbed red and blue color over her face, and handed it to George and John for them to do the same. Sarah, wrapped in a blanket, with her black hair hanging over her shoulders, looked just like a Bannock woman.

"Go ahead of me far enough that I can follow you to father's lodge," she told her brother. "I will go on foot. My men will stay here and watch the horses."

The mountain was rocky, very steep and hard to climb, even on hands and knees. At last, she reached the top and looked down into the great encampment, alive with angry Bannocks. For just an instant, she felt a twinge of fear, and yet it was a very beautiful sight, stretching far across the lowlands with little campfires scattered here and there. It was bustling with activity. Sarah could see many of the warriors catching their horses and riding away, and some of the women were cutting and cooking beef.

Lee came back to tell her the way to Winnemucca's lodge. She listened carefully, then said, "Go tell father I am coming. I will go on alone. We must hurry, for there is no time to lose."

Lee caught her by the shoulders and looked at her, great love and admiration in his eyes. "Please be careful, my sister."

"Do not worry. I will go very fast. We must not be afraid."

Running, dodging rocks, jumping off ridges and dropping to the ground at the least strange sound, Sarah at last reached Winnemucca's camp. She entered the wickiup and ran to her father, who took her in his arms.

"Oh, my dear little girl," he murmured. "You

should not have come. The danger is great." He raised his face toward heaven. "Oh, Father in the spirit-land, look down on us and help."

"Are you all right, father?" Sarah asked anxiously, looking at his lined and troubled face. "Are you strong enough to travel?"

"Yes, my daughter. But the Bannocks are keeping us prisoner. They do not watch us closely, but it would be hard for all of us to get away."

Sarah moved into the center of them so all present could hear her. "I have come from the soldier-fathers with word for you to leave this hostile camp and come to them. They will look after you. This is the plan, and we must whisper it among ourselves, go tell others and be very quiet about it. We must hurry." She looked at the chief. "Father, tell the women and children to make believe they are going out to gather wood, and to slip away by ones and twos. We will all meet at Juniper Lake."

The women, with their children close beside them, took ropes they used in gathering wood and began to leave, even as Sarah was talking. "We will need as many horses and ponies as we can get," she went on. "Traveling by foot will be too slow and the Bannocks will overtake us."

Chief Winnemucca instructed Lee to get as many horses and ponies as possible and drive them to the Lake. Lee left immediately, riding off quietly into the darkening evening light. Soon, others separated and made their own way across the mountain in a direction of the Lake.

Fleeing through wilderness, always keeping her father in sight, Sarah became tense when she heard a horse running behind them. She quickly dropped to the ground. The horse stopped close by and its rider gave the family whistle, and a young voice asked softly, "Father, where are you?"

It was Lee's wife Mattie. She had gone on with women and children, but had come back with a horse to help Chief Winnemucca reach the meeting place easier. She and Sarah embraced and then helped the chief mount.

When they reached John and George, who were waiting, Sarah sent them on ahead. She and Mattie ran down the rough mountainside hand-in-hand, with Winnemucca and others coming along behind.

The two Paiute scouts were waiting at Juniper Lake, and Indian women had cooked some mountain sheep meat. There had been so much to do and so many problems on her mind Sarah had forgotten all about eating, and even now, there was no time for it.

"Come, take some of the meat in your hands and get on your horses. We will eat while we ride, for we have a long way to go. Tie your children to your backs so if they sleep, they will not fall off. We must travel all the night through."

Seventy-five men, women and children had successfully crept away from the Bannocks that night. As they prepared to leave Juniper Lake, Lee came to Sarah and said, "I will go back. There are many more of our people who did not have a chance to get away. I will use these same tactics and lead them to you."

"Good," Sarah replied. "We will wait for you at Summit Springs." Then, she turned to Winnemucca. "I believe we are ready to ride. Give the orders, father."

Chief Winnemucca told his people, "Ride two by two! Keep close together! Men, stay close by your wives and children. Six braves keep back to see if we are being followed."

With the chief, Mattie and Sarah in the lead, this procession moved through the night without incident and at dawn arrived at Summit Springs.

"We will stop here for a while and wait for Lee, as we promised," Sarah said. "It will be a good time for rest."

They unsaddled their horses and all lay down to try to sleep. Sarah's eyes had barely closed when a runner galloped into camp, his horse exhausted and flecked with foam.

"We are followed!" he shouted. "Lee and band are overtaken!"

Sarah jumped up and ran to the top of a high ridge. In the far distance she saw Bannock warriors riding to overtake a small band of fleeing Paiutes. As she watched, guns fired and the leader fell from his horse.

"Lee!" she whispered under her breath.

Suddenly, she realized her father was standing beside her. "My son! If he is killed, I will go back to them and be killed also."

"Father!" Sarah said. "Do not talk nonsense. You are needed by our people more than ever now. Come, we must go! There is no time to be lost." She caught him by the arm and looked into his worried face. "Although my life is very precious to me, I would not hesitate a moment to lose it in trying to save yours."

Quickly, she gathered Paiutes around her. "I am going to ride on ahead to get help from the soldiers," Sarah told them. "They will listen to me because they know me, and there will be less risk."

"Yes, my daughter," the old chief agreed. "Tell them to send soldier-fathers to protect my people."

"Let me go with you," Mattie cried. "You should not go alone, and George and John are needed here to help."

"Come on!" Sarah told her. They mounted their horses and rode off at a gallop, skimming hills and valleys, to get help from the troops. They continued their fast pace as the sun climbed slowly higher and prayed to their Father in the spirit-land to watch over and protect their people.

Mattie had learned to speak English from Mrs. Parrish, and although she pronounced words slowly, her speech had a pretty musical quality. She made each sentence sound like a song and her phrases were like poetry. All through her short life, she made those around her happy with her kindness and sweet ways. Sarah made no mention of fears that Mattie's husband, Lee, had been killed. There was no need to bring sadness to this girl who was like her own sister, until she was sure.

In the afternoon, they stopped at Muddy Creek. While their horses drank and rested, they ate white currants from bushes growing near. Then the women found a narrow place to jump their horses across and continued on toward the soldiers.

They arrived at Sheep Ranch late that night and found General Howard there with his men. Sarah flung herself off her horse and ran to tell him, breathlessly, "My father is on his way with some of his people, but he needs help. Please, send some soldiers, at once."

Pi-Ute Joe was called in and Sarah told him where the fleeing Indians were. The general dispatched men to go with him immediately to rescue Chief Winnemucca. "Guide him with his party safely to Fort McDermit," were his orders.

As soon as the company of soldiers had gone, Sarah gave General Howard all information she had learned, exact location of the Bannock camp and their approximate strength. "I will make a guess there are over a thousand gathered there in the valley, with war bands coming and going all of the time."

"You have shown your usual bravery and courage," General Howard told her gratefully. "Now, you and Mattie must eat something and get some sleep."

Next morning, the general told Sarah they were moving on to Fort Lyon. "I would like for you to stay with us, and Mattie can come along, too, if she is not afraid."

"I am no coward-girl," Mattie told him proudly. "I am not afraid, even of the noise of guns. I do not like war, but I will go with my dear sister."

Sarah didn't enjoy the trip to Fort Lyon. For some reason, General Howard insisted the two women ride in a wagon, and she much preferred to travel horseback. Then, wounding her pride even more, on the way they met a group of citizen scouts and she overheard one of them say, "Oh, look! They have Sarah Winnemucca prisoner!" This made her very angry at first, but Mattie began to laugh and in a few minutes Sarah saw the funny side of it, too. Later, they told General Howard and the three of them made a good joke of the incident.

At old Fort Lyon, Sarah prevailed upon the general to let her ride horseback and they pushed on toward Fort Harney to join Captain Bernard, who was already there with his forces. There had been word that Bannocks had abandoned Steens Mountain and gone to Harney Valley, and citizen scouts continued to report hostiles ready and waiting to fight in the wooded hills just above the fort.

As they approached the military base, General Howard asked Sarah, "Do you think citizen scouts are right about the fort being in danger?"

"General," she replied, "if you find any Indians within two hundred miles of here, you may say Sarah is telling lies."

"Then, why would they make these reports?" he asked, puzzled.

"I do not know, but I will stake my life on it that they are wrong."

Later in the day, it all became clear. Sarah and Mattie were the first to notice the trick Indians had played. It was piling rocks on a high hill in such a fashion that it looked like men waiting there. The two women noticed and recognized this clever Indian trick at once, but Sarah whispered, "Say nothing. Let us wait and see what happens."

Sure enough, before long, a bugle sounded an order to halt, and a citizen scout came to General Howard on the run.

"Sir!" he shouted, his voice high and unnatural with fear. "Look! On that hill yonder! Don't you see the Indians?"

General Howard squinted his eyes and shaded them with his hand. He turned his head and stretched his neck first one way and then another, trying for a better look. "Yes," he said at last, "I do see something." He stood up a bit in his stirrups, still trying hard to see. "But—but I don't see them moving."

"Oh, I do, sir! They're getting in good position to fight us." He moved about nervously, wanting to run for cover. "They have a good place up there."

General Howard called to Sarah. "Look up there." He pointed. "Aren't those Indians? What have you got to say now?"

"The same as I said before," Sarah replied calmly. "I see nothing but some rocks put there to deceive you."

Citizen scouts dropped to the rear and officers gathered around the General, taking out their field glasses for a closer view.

"Sarah, that sure looks like Indians up there to me," one of them said. He handed her his binoculars. "Here, take a *good* look through these," he urged.

"I do not need these glasses," Sarah exclaimed, pushing them away. "There are no Indians there. I will go up there myself, just to show you I am telling the truth."

She started off at a gallop, but General Howard yelled at her. "Sarah! You'll be killed! Wait! Some men will go with you."

To please him, she waited for soldiers and when they got to the top of the ridge found everything just as she had told them.

"That is one way Indians do deceive the white people," Sarah explained. "We pile rocks, one on the other, and put a round one at the top to make it look like a man. This gives us time to get away from our enemies."

The whites learned that Indians had many ways of giving them the slip, which made keeping track of them a big problem during this war.

» 13

Sarah became military personnel without a uniform or official title, but still of great importance in this conflict with Indians. She wore durable calico dresses given to her by wives of army men living at the forts, and she covered them with a regulation army coat when the weather was cold. She kept her black hair parted in the middle, with two long braids reaching nearly to her waist. She was a neat and attractive figure going about her tasks and was well liked by everyone with whom she came in contact.

Her services consisted mainly of acting as a guide, counselor and messenger for troops, but she also helped to locate hostile bands of warriors and did her best to persuade them to stop fighting. Mattie, a cheerful companion and helper, stayed with her. She knew now her husband, Lee, had been wounded and maybe killed in a brief skirmish on the plains.

The Bannocks and their allies had descended into Oregon from the East in a bow-shaped pattern and quickly spread out through the countryside, leaving

"Indian Battle," an illustration by George Varian, from *Famous Indian Chiefs I Have Known* by O.O. Howard, published in 1912.

paths of destruction all along the way. Strangely enough, however, casualties on both sides were comparatively small because the army was directing its operations toward persuading red men to put down their weapons and surrender. They did not want to kill Indians; their main problem was to prevent tribes from uniting into a great mass of hostile enemies.

When news reached General Howard that nearly two thousand Bannocks were camped with their women and children on the north slope of the Blue Mountains near a divide between Butter and Birch Creeks, he became very concerned. He was afraid they were planning an assault on Fort Pendleton, and decided to strike first.

Sarah tried to dissuade him. "The Bannocks will have the best of it," she said. "They have timber on their side and can find places to hide in the woods."

"But we cannot just sit here and do nothing while they are planning an attack," the general argued. He went ahead with his plans, joining Bernard's cavalry, and in the early morning hours, they advanced over the rough and rugged ground, and moved quickly into position.

From a high slope at the rear of the troops where they sat on their horses, Sarah and Mattie watched unhappily. To Sarah, it was like a bad dream, and she had a great lump in her throat, as if she wanted to cry.

"I do not know if I can stand it," she told Mattie. "I am afraid we will see many of our people killed today, and soldiers, too. And for what good? I wish I could stop them!"

The bugle sounded 'Fire!' Sarah closed her eyes, hearing nothing but the thunder of big guns, the pounding of horses' hooves and the wild war whoops of Indians. She tightened her grip on the reins of her horse and forced her eyes open. She immediately stiffened with shock. The first ones she saw were Oytes and Egan, circling the front lines, their faces wild and strange as they yelled defiance to white soldiers.

"I must go to them," Sarah knew at once. "I can make them stop. I know I can!"

Superior fire power of the soldiers pushed Indians back. As troops advanced, red men abandoned their first positions and retreated to the next height, using lava rock as a shield. Bullets whistled through the air as soldiers pursued them. Hostiles struck for thick pines and again made a stand, using trees for protection. The chiefs kept circling and chanting and whooping, exposing themselves to gunfire in an effort to encourage their warriors.

General Howard looked around and saw Sarah and Mattie staring at the battle, unprotected. "Take cover," he ordered. "Get behind some rocks, quickly!"

Mattie obeyed at once, but Sarah moved her horse along side the general. "Let me go to the front lines," she begged. "I will make Egan and Oytes hear me. They will listen to reason. I know they will!"

"No, Sarah, not this time," General Howard told her sternly. "It's much too dangerous. You'll be killed."

"Please, general! I am not afraid! I will try to make peace with Indians. Those two chiefs, Egan and Oytes, I know them like my brothers. They do not want to make war; they have been pushed into it. Let me try, general. Please!" Sarah begged.

General Howard could not stand up against her fervent pleas, and finally said, "All right, Sarah, go on. But try to be careful."

She put the whip to her horse and galloped to the front lines. She called out to Indians she knew when they sped by, but in the dust and confusion and noise, they couldn't see her nor could they hear her and her cries grew more and more desperate as she realized she couldn't reach them.

Indians were pushed further and futher back into the mountains, and by midday had made a hasty retreat, leaving camp supplies and many horses behind. General Howard rode over beside Sarah, a disconsolate little figure with a look of despair on her face.

"You and Mattie may go with soldiers into the woods to look for any wounded Indians who need help," he told her sympathetically.

Everything seemed unnaturally still after the noise of this battle, as Mattie and Sarah, with a detachment of army men, searched among trees and brush for dead and wounded. They found none, but when they went to investigate a faint mewing sound in a patch of thick undergrowth, they discovered a Bannock baby, lying on its face in pine needles. It had evidently fallen unnoticed from its cradle basket as hostiles had scrambled out of the area in great haste to get away from soldiers' guns. Mattie picked the baby up in gentle arms and took it back to camp. All they had to feed it were ginger snaps and water until General Howard managed to get some milk for the hungry infant.

"Take good care of its little yellow shirt and all of its beads," he told Sarah. "When this war is over we will find its mother."

Next day, they came across two Indian women who had returned to pick up food which had been left behind. Sarah told them about the baby, and they agreed to stay with the troops and care for it until a better home for the child could be found.

For a long time afterward, the sight of this battle, with Egan and Oytes behaving like hostiles, was constantly on Sarah's mind. Finally, she confided to Mattie, "Do you think it strange that with all those splendid firearms and the Gatling Gun they are so proud of, and the air full of bullets that not an Indian fell in battle? We found no dead or wounded Indians and only a few soldiers were hurt."

"Paiutes do not kill soldier-fathers if they can help it," Mattie agreed. "They like them too well. But I am surprised at Oytes—and most of all at Egan. How disappointed our father would have been to see them."

"Yes," Sarah said, shaking her head sadly. "But they were made to do it. Things Agent Rinehart did at the reservation were more than they could stand. I cannot blame them, although it makes my heart ache to see them in war and yelling defiance to the army."

By the end of July, hostile Indians were thinning out of Oregon, but soldiers still kept up the chase. General Howard and Captain Bernard, with their troops, continued across steep and treacherous trails of the Blue Mountain Range, down into Granite Creek Valley and on to the Ironside area.

When they camped at an intersection of Canyon City and Malheur Reservation wagon roads, General Howard asked Sarah to ride into the reservation to see if any of her people were there. She found it deserted, but met some of her father's band from McDermit who told her the glad news that her brother, Lee, was still alive.

"He was wounded, but escaped when Bannock forces weakened. He is at McDermit with Chief Winnemucca, but has plans to look for you and Mattie when he is stronger."

Sarah's eyes filled with happy tears. "Tell Lee and my father we are safe and well and we will all be together soon."

In September, the Bannock War came to an end. General Howard assigned Sarah and Mattie to the task of helping troops bring in small bands of Indians, acting as interpreters and guides.

"Take them to McDermit where the army can take care of them," were his instructions.

The night before they were to leave, a rider galloped into camp. Still nervous and alert, a sentry put his gun to the ready and challenged the horseman. "I am Lee Winnemucca," came a voice from the darkness. "I have come to find my wife and my sister."

There was great rejoicing as the three were reunited after so many long and dangerous months. Lee was thin and wan, but happiness at being with Mattie and Sarah once again made his dark eyes glow and brought a flush to his thin cheeks.

General Howard came forward and shook Lee's

hand. "It is good to see you, my friend," he said. "I have asked your wife and Sarah to go with Lieutenant Colonel Forsyth to find Indians who may be needing help. Perhaps you could go along. I feel you would be of great help to us—and to them."

Lee agreed, and for the next month, the three of them were assigned to help with this important work. One time, when they were only seventy miles from Fort McDermit, Sarah asked the colonel if she could go and see her father and then rejoin his troops the next day at Antelope Springs.

"Of course you can," he told her. "And I'll send an escort with you."

"Oh, no, there is no need of that," she protested. "I will be riding at night and can get there faster if I go by myself."

Colonel Forsyth didn't know Sarah as well as some of the other army officers and he would not hear of her going alone. He sent Lieutenant Pitcher and two soldiers with her as escort, and they started late in the evening. To Sarah's great disappointment they traveled at a slow, cautious pace, not getting their horses out of a trot all night long.

In the early morning hours, before dawn, Lieutenant Pitcher had to stop to fix his saddle, and Sarah asked if she could ride on ahead. When he gave his consent, she took off at once. It was a great relief to her to be riding fast and she arrived at Fort McDermit at daybreak.

There were nearly six hundred camps spread out across the prairie. Sarah stopped at one and awakened the Indians by shouting, "Here! You are sleeping too much!"

One of the women jumped up, her eyes wide with surprise and fear. "What is it?" she cried. "Who are you?" Then, she recognized the princess of her tribe and her face broke into a broad smile. "It is our dear Shellflower," she called to the others.

"Where is the camp of my family?" Sarah asked.

"Your brother, Natchez, is here, next to us."

Sarah remained for a moment longer, speaking with her old friends, and then went on quietly to the next camp.

"Halloo!" she called out loudly. "The enemy is at hand!"

Natchez sat up quickly and looked at her, frowning. He shook his head, looked again, as if he couldn't believe his eyes. "My sister," he said softly, and then shouted, "My sister!" He jumped up to help Sarah off her horse. "Get up, wife! Make a fire. My sister is here. She is cold."

He brought a blanket and put it around her shoulders. Soon, the fire was glowing and they sat around it, holding out their hands to its warmth. Natchez sent runners to spread the news. "Tell them I have in my camp a warrior who has just arrived. They must all come to see for themselves who it is."

Chief Winnemucca got there first. He went to Sarah and took her tenderly in his arms. "Oh, my poor child, my poor child!" he murmured over and over again.

Sarah snuggled her head into his shoulder, and it was just as comforting as it had always been, for as long as she could remember. When her father said, "Look up, my child, and let me see if it is really you," she saw tears running down his wrinkled face. Everyone cried, but it was for joy.

They talked for a long time, with Sarah telling them what she had seen and done since the last time they were all together. She hesitated to tell them a bit of news she had heard just a few days before, because she knew it would throw a damper on their happiness.

At last, taking her father's hand in hers, she said solemnly, "It makes my heart sad to tell you that Egan is dead. He was not killed by soldiers, or even by white men, unless one of them was responsible for starting the rumor among Indians that the government would pay a thousand dollars for Egan's head. It was Umapine, a cruel and wicked Umatilla scout, who killed our friend, thinking he would get a reward for it." She sighed. "It is because of things like this that we are trying to get all of our people in from the mountains. They need to be where our soldier-fathers can look after them and protect them from greed and wickedness of men like Umapine."

Winnemucca had listened to all of the talk in silence. Then, he raised his hand and spoke to his people. "I grieve for our brother Egan, as I have grieved ever since he took the path to war. I thank the spirit-father that my dear daughter was spared to return to us. Her name has now gone far beyond ours; none of us can ever come up to her great deeds. Her name is everywhere, and everyone praises her. Hereafter, we will look upon her as our chieftain, for none of us is worthy of being chief but her."

The people nodded their heads and murmured reverently, "Shellflower is brave, and her heart is good."

Sarah's army escorts finally arrived and she traveled on with them to Antelope Springs, as she had promised the colonel.

The soldiers proceeded, but were able to go only forty miles further since many horses were worn out and needed rest. They camped in a deep canyon at a place called "Three Forks of the Owyhee River."

That night, around the campfire, Lee told of an experience he'd had at this place several years before. "We were on that hill yonder, and soldiers were on that steep mountain just across from it. They had a mule with a wagon gun strapped to its back. The soldiers were new to this part of the country and were very nervous about Indians. We could tell. So, we called out to them. They stopped, and some of them tried to hide. We found this to be very funny, so we all started calling out to them again. By then, they were so frightened they shot at us." Lee went off into a spasm of laughter, while others looked at him wonderingly.

"It was funny for soldiers to shoot at you?" Mattie finally asked.

"Oh, no, not that. What was funny, they fired the gun before they took it off the mule's back, and it knocked the poor old fellow down. He rolled over and over, down the steep mountain. The soldiers all took out after their disappearing gun and mule, yelling and shouting for him to stop, but the mule kept rolling faster all the time." He broke off, laughing again, but this time the others laughed with him.

"Some of our people said that if the soldiers were going to shoot mules at us, we had better go away, so we went on all night without stopping."

When Colonel Forsyth and his soldiers got to Silver City, he had orders to divide his command. Captain Bernard was to turn south and bring together Indians who might be in the neighborhood of Duck Valley, Harney and the region between there and McDermit. Sarah went with him, while Lee and Mattie rounded up Indians who still remained around Silver City and took them to the McDermit post.

When Sarah arrived at Camp Harney, she found a great many Bannocks there and sent for the baby they had found after the battle at Birch Creek. She also got its little yellow shirt and beads General Howard had advised her to keep, and made the rounds.

In one camp, she found a young Indian couple weeping over an empty cradle and felt she had found the right place. "I have here a little girl baby who was lost on the battlefield and I am trying to find her father and mother. It is a Bannock child. I have also her shirt and beads."

The young parents ran to her and the mother clasped the child to her bosom, crying over and over, "My baby! My baby!"

"We have great thanks in our hearts for you," the Bannock brave said to Sarah. "You have saved our little girl!"

» 14

In October, an order came from Washington stating the Indians who were originally from Malheur should be gathered together at Camp Harney and from there be taken back to Malheur Reservation for the winter. Sarah had instructions to bring all of her people from McDermit and surrounding area to Harney. Lee and Mattie went with her. She was unable to quiet uneasiness among the Paiutes about this move, however, because, in truth, she didn't understand it herself.

"We do not want to go to Malheur," they told her. "There is something wrong."

Sarah explained to them their soldier-fathers had word from Washington to do this, and Indians would be cared for at Malheur. With some misgivings, she assured them they had nothing to fear.

In spite of his daughter's reassurances, Chief Winnemucca announced he would stay on with soldiers at McDermit. He appointed a Paiute leader called "Leggins" to be in charge of those of his band who wished to go with Sarah to Harney and then on to

Malheur Reservation.

There were quite a number of Winnemucca's band who decided to go and after a time talked of getting back to their old home. They hoped Rinehart would not be there, but instead, another good agent-father like Mr. Parrish. Within a week, they were at Harney, waiting for further orders.

Then, one day in December, without warning, a blow fell. Major Cochran sent for Sarah and told her, "I have some bad news for you, but do not say anything about it to your people until we see if something can be done."

"What now?" Sarah wondered uneasily. "What new misfortune is about to befall my people?" Aloud, she said, "You know I will not say anything you want kept secret, but something tells me this is bad."

"Yes, it is," he admitted. "Another order has come for your people to be taken north to the Yakima Reservation, across the Columbia River."

Sarah felt the blood drain from her face. *"All* of my people?"

"Not your father and ones with him at McDermit, nor the ones of his band who came here with Leggins, but all others who are here must go."

"But why?" Sarah cried. "Why my people? They have done nothing wrong. Why should they be sent away from their own country into a strange land?"

"I have no idea," the officer admitted. "It doesn't make sense to me either."

"Is there anything you can do?" Sarah asked. "If anyone is to be sent away, it should be Oytes and his men and the Bannocks who are with them. They fought against the soldiers; these other Paiutes did not. Oh, sir, if you knew how I have promised them they would be treated fairly by soldier-fathers, you would leave nothing undone to help them."

"Keep up a good heart, Sarah," he replied. "I'll write directly to the President of the United States, and see if we can keep them here."

With great sorrow, Sarah remarked, "My people will stop trusting me if this is done, and I am the only one they have to 'talk' for them. They will believe I am the one who lied instead of the government. They will believe I am working against them just like reservation agents and getting money for betraying and cheating them."

"No, Sarah, they will never believe that," the officer declared. "Your people love you. They know all you ever think about is how you can help them."

That evening, Sarah wearily walked around the area. She found Indians singing in various camps and heard sounds of joyous laughter. "My poor people," she thought to herself and returned to headquarters for a sleepless night.

Days dragged by and Sarah had about given up on a reply to Major Cochran's letter to Washington. However, when the officer sent for her one morning, she felt sure an answer *had* come and the news would not be good. Dismally, she said to Mattie, "I wish this was my last day in this cruel world!"

"Oh, no, Sarah, you do not mean that!" Mattie gasped.

"No, I guess I do not mean exactly that. I guess I mean my last day with the cruel, cruel, wicked white people who want to drive us away to some foreign land." She stood up, hesitated a moment and sat down again. "I do not believe I can walk to the office."

Mattie came to her side at once. "You have taken all of this so much to heart you have made yourself sick," she scolded Sarah gently. "Come, I will go with you to learn if the news is good or bad."

When Major Cochran opened his door to them, he stared at the Indian princess with a shocked expression. "Sarah! Are you sick?" he asked quickly.

"Heartsick," she replied and sat down.

"She grieves about our people," Mattie explained.

"Yes, I know." The officer walked over to his desk and picked up a long, official-looking letter. "And there seems to be nothing I can do to help. The order which came in this letter today from President Rutherford B. Hayes says your people must be moved to Yakima Reservation. I'm sorry, Sarah."

"This is unbelievable," Sarah cried. "What kind of man is this president to send my people with their old ones and many little children out in the bitter cold and snow? Or is he a man at all? He must be a beast with no heart at all in his breast!" Sarah got up and walked to a window. She looked out over the great encampment, tears stinging her eyes, and then turned back to the officer.

"I have never seen a president in my life, but I cannot believe he is a human being. No one made of flesh and blood would send anyone across those fearful mountains in midwinter!"

"I feel a great shame for my countrymen and our leader," Major Cochran confessed. "What they are doing is not right, and I cannot blame you for saying harsh things about them."

Yet, the hardest thing Sarah had to do was tell her people they were being sent to Yakima Reservation. As she feared, some of them muttered angrily that their Shellflower had become like white people, full of lies and deception. But most of them knew Sarah would not have misled them if she, herself, had not been deceived.

It was only a short while until Christmas, and the tribes were given but one week to get ready. Sarah and Mattie gathered up all the furs they could find from army supplies. There were fur caps, fur gloves, overshoes trimmed with fur, and heavy blue coats. They issued these to the Indians who stood around fires, wailing their grief to the winter skies.

As soon as they heard where they were to be taken, many of the Paiutes tried to slip away. One afternoon, Sarah and Mattie were sent out to get some who had left. It was cold and icy, and the ground was treacherous underfoot. Even though both women were good riders, they were traveling very fast when Mattie's horse slipped and threw her. She fell hard, but went on with Sarah, even though suffering agonizing pain, to help talk the Indians into coming back to camp.

Fifty wagons, with citizens hired to drive them, transported Paiutes to their new home. The caravan had gone no further than Canyon City when yet another message came from Washington. It ordered Leggins and his band also to be taken to Yakima Reservation. The travelers had to wait there two days in a howling blizzard, and snow continued to fall on them the rest of the way.

Death and misery marked the long, hard trip. Babies were born and babies died. Young mothers died for lack of care. Little children froze to death in the below-zero temperature. The cold, combined with desperation and grief, became too much for many old ones. Some of the bodies were put under the snow, but others were merely dumped by the roadside and left behind.

The five hundred and forty-three Indians who survived this tragic journey were met by Agent Wilbur and a Yakima Chief some thirty miles from agency buildings, where they had to camp for ten days. It seemed Agent Wilbur had frantically tried to stop the official order which sent them there for he had no place to put them. Also, native Indians resented the new-comers crowding in.

Agent Wilbur asked Sarah if she would act as interpreter for her people and she said she would. After a time, the weary travelers were put into some long, narrow sheds with no wood for fires and snow piled all around outside, three feet deep. Paiutes were cold and some of them became ill.

It didn't take Sarah long to find out that the man who served Yakima Reservation as a doctor had no compassion at all for these suffering people. When she went to him for medicine, more often than not, he would say, "Well, Sarah, I'll give you a little sugar and rice, or maybe some tea." With a laugh which infuriated her almost to violence, he would add, "We'll give them something good to eat before they die."

Many of the Paiutes did die that winter and spring. One of them was little Mattie. Never as strong and robust physically as members of Sarah's family, and not fully recovered from her fall, she could not endure the cold and privations of this life they were forced to lead. She became very ill soon after their arrival at the reservation, and steadily weakened, in spite of all Sarah and Lee could do. At last, holding fast to her husband's hand, she closed her eyes and was gone.

Sarah had never felt such bitterness and hatred as when she helped her brother scoop out a resting place for Mattie underneath the deep snow. "Brave little Mattie," she said through her tears. "She survived the war but was not strong enough to overcome things the white man does to us."

The Nevada Paiutes were constantly harassed by Yakima Indians who did not want them around. The few horses and ponies Leggins and his band had brought disappeared, and blankets were stolen off women and children as they slept. Yakima braves taunted Paiutes into gambling and won most of their clothing. The small amount of food issued to them was usually contaminated, for they could not buy rations as the Yakimas could.

Indians from Nevada had no money, nor any way to earn it, nor did they have anywhere to go to gather food for themselves. Sarah asked Mrs. Wilbur why it was necessary for Indians to have money to buy food since the government sent it with clothing and blankets to be issued to them free of charge. The woman told her they had to sell them in order to keep their job. Thus, Sarah could only assume someone in a higher position was getting a large portion of the "blood money" extracted from Indians.

She wanted to go to Washington and actually talk to some of the men who so callously moved her people here and there, like pawns on a playing board. She wanted to tell someone in really high echelons of the government just how Indians were cheated out of things that were rightfully theirs, or made to pay in order to get them. "Just as soon as I get some of my military pay," she promised the Paiutes, "I am going to Washington, and I will talk."

While she was waiting for her money, she wrote a letter to secretary of the Interior, Carl Schurz, telling him of the sorry condition of Paiutes at Yakima Reservation. She asked him to please send them some food and supplies. She did not receive an answer, nor did any food or supplies come.

In July, Agent Wilbur informed Sarah they were going to have a camp meeting at the agency and there would be some important visitors from the East. "Please keep that ragged, scraggly bunch of yours out of sight," he told her. "We don't want to be embarrassed."

How little he knew Sarah Winnemucca! She coached her people well. The meeting had scarcely gotten underway when she marched in with these Nevada Indians, some of them half naked and all of them thin and haggard. They sat down on the very front row so the eastern visitors could get a good view of them and see how Paiutes were treated.

Agent Wilbur was furious. He called Sarah into his office and gave her a severe reprimand for her conduct.

"You will not have to worry with me much longer," she told him in a cutting tone. "As soon as I get my government money I am going to Washington to speak for the Paiutes. And never fear, your name will be mentioned quite often!"

She was certain Agent Wilbur was glad to see her go, but her threat had not been an idle one. Still fresh in her mind was the terrible winter just passed and the bitter knowledge that none of it was necessary and could have been avoided.

She bade her people good-by and went first to Vancouver to talk with General Howard. She told him everything, trying not to weep when she recounted the story of Mattie's death. When she had finished, he sat silent for a long time, his face thoughtful and full of sorrow.

"I am sorry, Sarah," he said at last. "And I feel guilty as all my race should. I have tried to help as much as I can, but not too many white people feel as I do."

"I want to go to Washington and talk for the Paiutes. I will—I will do anything to help. But I fear officials are all against me because I speak the truth." She thought hard for a moment. "And no place on earth is more filled with government officials than Washington. What do you think I should do?"

"You have been of great service to our country," General Howard said. "Government officials should at least listen to you."

"But do you think they will? Up to now, officials have done their best to keep me still."

"That is true." The General wrinkled his forehead in deep thought. "Maybe you should take your story straight to the people," he suggested at last, the light of a new idea beginning to shine in his eyes. "Yes, that's it. I have a friend who is a newspaperman in San Francisco. His name is Parker. He covered news of the Bannock War." General Howard smiled broadly. "You may remember him. He's the one who tied everything he could find which belonged to Indians on the mane and tail of his horse. Do you recall?"

"Oh, yes, now I do." She joined in the laughter. "One day citizen scouts took a shot at him and nearly scared him to death. I told him it was no wonder with all those feathers and beads and red rags on his horse. They took him for a blue-eyed Indian."

"That makes it easier since he knows you already and is familiar with your work," the general said, serious again. "I will write to him about your coming, and I will also give you letters of introduction which will open some other doors for you."

When Sarah left, the general walked to the door with her, beaming. "This may be the very thing, Sarah. Rottenness can't thrive on fresh air, and snakes, especially two-legged ones, won't like the bright glare of publicity."

When Sarah arrived in San Francisco, Parker met her and pumped her hand up and down energetically. "It's not often we have a genuine Indian princess in our town, and you're going to get a lot of publicity in our paper."

Parker was true to his word and also helped her to get speaking engagements with civic clubs, social organizations and women's meetings.

In her native Paiute costume, the attractive Indian princess told the truth about government promises which were made and never kept, injustices like sending peaceful Paiutes out of their own territory and into an overcrowded reservation as Yakima, and the unbelievable conditions on Indian reservations in general. She emphasized the cruel and dishonest policies of Indian agents, naming in particular Rinehart and Wilbur, who had dragged her people down into extremest poverty. She did not hesitate to call names of men in the Indian Bureau from the highest official on down to the lowest, and none of them showed up to challenge her statements.

Her beauty and sincerity made a tremendously favorable impression on the public. She was in great demand as a speaker, and her lectures started a wave of sympathy for Indians rolling throughout the West which government officials could not ignore.

"Now is the time to go to Washington," Sarah decided.

When she told Mr. Parker of her plans, he wrote a big story for distribution to all western papers, telling how the Paiute princess was heading for the East to continue her lectures. He also notified Washington newsmen she was planning to be in their area soon.

On her way to the capital city, Sarah stopped in Nevada for a few days to see her family and found her father and Natchez with their tribes in Lovelock Valley. It was here she told the lean, hungry and ragged Paiutes, in answer to their pleas, that she was going to go to the East to talk for them. And it was here she had received the telegram from Special Agent Haworth, summoning her, together with her father and brother, to Washington. With what high hopes she had set out.

» 15

It seemed a long time to Sarah since she, Chief Winnemucca and Natchez, with Special Agent Haworth, had left the sage country for Washington. Their talks with Secretary Schurz, the short interview with President Hayes and the long hours of sightseeing in the nation's capital city were all in the past now. The Indian princess, as well as her father and brother, were happy to be back in the wide open spaces of Nevada once more.

Every so often on the long trip home, Sarah had taken out her copy of Mr. Schurz's order to release Paiutes from Yakima Reservation and read it through, just to make certain the wonderful words were really there. She guarded it as carefully as if it were something of great worth. To Sarah, it was.

The first thing she did when they got off the train was to wire Secretary Schurz they were in Lovelock, Nevada, and for him to send the supplies he had promised as soon as possible. Then, without delay, Sarah rode out through the area, telling all Paiutes to come to Lovelock to get their share of supplies the

Department of Interior would send.

Paiutes, in turn, went to one another, spreading this happy news. Indians from all over Nevada gathered in the valley, anxious to receive tents and clothing and food. They were also anxious to hear of their great White Father in Washington, direct from the lips of Sarah Winnemucca. They wanted to know how he looked, what clothes he wore, what his wickiup was like and what words he had spoken to their three people to bring home to them.

Sarah told them all of these things while they waited for supplies to come. She told them of the interesting sights they had seen in Washington, and answered all questions about their White Father. But soon everything was told, and days passed, and no supplies came. It was cold and the snow was deep and Indians had nothing to eat.

With growing fear in her heart, Sarah again wired Secretary Schurz, "For God's sake; send us some food!" The only reply she received to this urgent request was a terse message, "Take your people to Malheur Reservation."

Sarah sank to her knees, holding the telegram in shaking fingers. She wondered if Mr. Schurz knew that Malheur was three hundred miles away. Too, General Howard had told her Rinehart was still there—that he had stayed all during the Bannock War drawing his salary although the reservation was deserted. Even if she could get her people there, what good would it do?

In despair Sarah broke down and cried hysterically. How could people she had talked with in Washington be so callous and unfeeling! They had looked her in the eye and told her lies. She supposed Secretary Schurz had never intended to send supplies at all. They only wanted to be rid of a woman they considered to be a nuisance. The bitterest hurt of all, though, to Sarah, was that in trusting officials in Washington, she had told her people a lie.

When able to control herself, she called the Paiutes

together and told them there would be no supplies. "Officials in Washington told me lies, and I believed them," she sobbed.

Through murmurs of dismay, Sarah could hear some saying, "We are not surprised. The great White Father is just like all white people." Yet, others said, "Thocmetony just made that up herself. Great White Father does not tell lies, surely."

"What I am telling you is the truth," Sarah kept repeating over and over. "They promised to send supplies and I believed them. I would not have told you if I had not thought it true."

A Paiute leader, called Captain John, who had come to hear about the White Father in Washington, rose slowly and spoke to the assembled Indians. "My dear people, I have lived many years with white people," he said. "Yes, it is over thirty years, and I know many of them, and never have I known one of them to do what they promised. I think they mean to do it at the time, but I tell you they are very forgetful. It seems to me, sometimes, that their memory is not good, and since I have come to understand them, if they say to me 'I will do so and so for you,' I say to them, 'Now or never.' Then, if they do not do it, I know it is because they never meant to do it, but only to say so. These are our white brothers' *ways,* and they are a weak people."

When he had finished speaking, Chief Winnemucca stood, and looked at Paiutes with sad eyes. "I do not blame you for feeling as you do," he said. "But do not have dark thoughts in your heart for your dear little Shellflower. I say, my children, that every word she has told you was said to her. And they have said more than this. They have talked on a paper which she has with her. She will tell you of it."

"I will read from the paper given to me by Secretary Schurz," Sarah told them. Indians grew very quiet and listened attentively to every word:

The Pi-Utes, heretofore entitled to live on the Malheur Reservation, their primeval home, are to have lands allotted to them in severalty, at the rate of one hundred and sixty acres to each head of a family, and each adult male. Such lands they are to cultivate for their own benefit. The allotment will be made under instructions of their agent. As soon as enabled by law to do so, this department is to give to the Indians patents for each tract of land conveying to each occupant the fee-simple in the lot he occupies.

Those of the Pi-Utes who in consequence of the Bannock War, went to the Yakima Reservation, and whoever may desire to rejoin their relatives, are at liberty to do so, without expense to the government for transportation. Those who desire to stay upon the Yakima Reservation and become permanently settled there will not be disturbed.

None of the Pi-Utes now living among the whites, and earning wages by their own work, will be compelled to go to the Malheur Reservation. They are at perfect liberty to continue working for wages for their own benefit, as they are now doing.

It is well understood that those who settle on the Malheur Reservation will not be supported by the government in idleness. They will be aided in starting their farms and promoting their civilization, but the support given them by the government will, according to law, depend upon their intelligence and efficiency in working for themselves.

C. Schurz,
Secretary of the Interior.

Sarah explained this order to them carefully, going into detail about its meaning. "We will all have to work, as we did when our Father Parrish lived with us, but we liked that."

They then talked among themselves, remembering the good times when Agent Parrish had been with them.

"Do you understand what the secretary of the Interior told us he would do?" she asked. "Is this all right with you?"

"If it is truth," Paiutes said, "it is all right."

"Can our people come home now, right away?" asked one.

"That is what the paper says," Sarah replied.

"It may be they can be back by the 'early-flowers-in-the-valley-time'," an old one whispered.

"Yes, it may be so," another answered, her wrinkled face wreathed in smiles, forgetting the snow and cold.

"But white people tell lies." Doubts began again. "They do not tell truth."

"Surely the talk on this paper which little Shell-flower read to us will come true."

Chief Winnemucca held up his hand and spoke, "Time will tell."

Before Paiutes left Lovelock to go back to their scattered camps, the old chief, who had put his army clothing on again, called them together once more.

"Here!" he said to one and all, holding out his white man's suit—a gift from the United States government. "Take it! This is all we can be sure of getting from our Big Father in Washington. I do not care for it. If our soldier-fathers had given it to me, I would keep it."

Not long after this meeting, Sarah received another telegram from Secretary Schurz, appointing her interpreter once again at the Malheur Agency in Oregon. Many questions arose in her mind. Had Rinehart been replaced at last? Had, perhaps, the promised supplies been sent there instead of Lovelock? It seemed reasonable.

In an effort to get scattered Paiutes together Sarah rode throughout Nevada, going from camp to camp, asking if they would go to Malheur.

"Bring our people back from Yakima, and then we will go to Malheur," she heard over and over again.

So, on the first of April, 1880, the Indian woman started north toward Yakima Reservation with the copy of Secretary Schurz's release order tucked safely in her saddlebag. She believed, since it was an official order, signed by the secretary himself, she would have no trouble getting her people together and bringing them home.

Very late on the third day, Sarah rode into a heavy mountain storm. Remembering a friendly white family who lived in the area, she picked her way through flying snowflakes to their ranchhouse.

A man opened the door and peered out at her. "Who are you?" he asked.

"I am Sarah Winnemucca, and am on my way to Yakima Reservation," she told him.

"Come on in," he said cordially. "You are welcome!" He led her over to the roaring fire to warm herself and sent one of his Indian hired hands to take her horse to the stable. Then he called his wife and family to meet the daughter of the chief they had always liked so well.

Next morning, the ranchers insisted the Indian princess remain with them until the storm was over. Snow was deep on the ground and more still falling. "You can lose your way easily out there," they told her, "even an experienced guide like yourself. Besides, we like to have company."

It was two days before the storm let up enough for her to proceed on her way. They had been days full of good talk, warm nourishing food and comfortable rest. But Sarah was eager to get on with her assignment.

When she reached Camp Harney she had to stop again because her horse was lame, but she couldn't continue on anyway for the Blue Mountains were impassable because of deep snow.

Captain Drury and other officers she knew greeted Sarah joyfully, and were very pleased with the order from Secretary Schurz which would allow Paiutes held at Yakima to return to Nevada.

As soon as a mountain trail was open, Captain Drury gave Sarah a government horse to ride. "Tell the mail carrier to bring it back," he said.

At Canyon City she took the stage, which was really only a buckboard wagon accommodating two passengers and the driver. Since it made only one trip a week, Sarah was delayed again and it was the first of May before she arrived at The Dalles, on the rapids of the Columbia River. There, she hired a horse for the two-day ride to Yakima Reservation. The nearer she got, the more jubilant she felt. "At last," she sang to herself, "I am bringing good news to my people. How happy they are going to be!"

Weary, yet happy herself, Sarah dismounted at agency headquarters as darkness crept along the lowlands. Agent Wilbur came out and seemed very surprised to see her.

"What do you want?" he asked.

"I have come a long way to talk to you," she replied. "May I come in?" He nodded and motioned her inside.

"You have received a letter from Washington. That is why I am here," she told him.

He leaned against his desk, looking down at her. "I've received no letter from Washington."

Sarah frowned, puzzled. "That is strange. They told me they had written, and that was some months ago."

"Who is this 'they' you're talking about?"

"The secretary of the Interior, Mr. Schurz. I visited with him in Washington and he wrote you a letter and gave me a copy of it. It concerns my people who are here."

"I haven't heard from anyone in Washington," Wilbur repeated. "You must be dreaming."

Sarah got her copy of the order from her saddlebag and with trembling hands held it out to the government agent. "I have here a copy of the letter which the Secretary gave me. Read it, and you will see it was not just a dream."

Wilbur scanned the paper hurridly. "I have not heard from anyone in Washington," he told her again, "and I cannot accept a carbon copy of one as an official order."

Sarah was stunned. She could not believe that she had been lied to about this, too. There had to be some mistake. This was too big—too important.

"But—but I came to take them home," she faltered.

"No, I can't permit it. I have no such orders to let them go."

Tears welling in her eyes, Sarah turned and went out into the night. A gust of cold wind swept across the lonely, open land as she stumbled toward her horse and leaned heavily for a moment against the warm side of the animal.

"Dear Grandfather in the spirit-land," she sobbed, "please, oh please, give me the strength and courage and knowledge to keep up the fight against this cruel, powerful world of your white brothers."

Sarah mounted and sat for a time thinking. She felt sure Lee would be camped on the range, caring for the agent's cattle. She galloped off into the white moonlight to find him.

Lee Winnemucca was on a lonely hillside, hunched over a fire in a ragged blanket. As Sarah approached, he looked up, and it struck at her heart to see her handsome brother looking so dejected and haggard.

Lee recognized her and got up to help her dismount. "Oh, my dear sister," he exclaimed as she gave him a big hug, "you have come back at last. Did you see the great White Father? It is so long we have waited for you."

"Yes, I saw him," she replied wearily. "Let me sit by your fire and rest. I have come a long way and have met with a great disappointment."

Then, she told her brother everything, and about this latest crisis which she could not accept as being final. "Dear brother, our people will never know what I have tried to do for them because they will not believe me any more. I am heartsick. For the life of me, I cannot even face them."

"Then stay here with me until you have thought it through," Lee suggested. "I have built a shelter over against the slope."

Sarah slept that night on the hard ground and all next day sat by a campfire, mulling over the problem which faced her, while Lee went about his work on the range.

In the dusky twilight, five Paiute men came trudging toward the fire and greeted their princess. Somehow, they had learned she was there and that she carried a paper with her from the great White Father in Washington. They demanded she return to camp with them. Lee went along for he sensed a hostility in their actions toward his sister.

» 16

When they arrived, a large group of Indians were assembled but not one got up to greet Sarah joyously as was usually the case when she returned after a long absence. Instead, Chief Leggins stood and began to speak.

"My dear children, you can see for yourselves that what we heard is true. Our little Shellflower is here, but she does not want to let us know what our White Father in Washington has done for us. We have no friend now. She first sold us to Father Wilbur and had us brought here, and now she has sold us to this bad man again to starve us." His voice quavered. "Oh, we shall never see our loved ones any more. There is nobody to talk for us now; we are all alone. We shall never get back to our sweet country."

"No! No!" Sarah cried out. "That is not true. Please—listen—."

Lee jumped up and shouted, "For shame! Are you all mad? Did any of you speak with Father Wilbur before you turned against my sister—your friend? He is the one who does not want us to go back! Not her!"

Sarah stood beside her brother and held the copy of Mr. Schurz's order high, so everyone could see. "I have suffered everything but death to come here with this paper. Now, I do not know if it speaks truth or not.

"You can say what you like about me. You have a right to say I have sold you, because that is the way it looks. I have said many things to you as the truth which were not my own words, but words of government officials. Because of this, I have told you more lies than I have hair on my head, but I tell you, my dear ones, I have never told you a lie which was made of my own words. They were promises made to me by white people.

"It is my dearest hope that you may see your loved ones again back in your own country. While I was in Washington, I said everything I could in your behalf and so did my father and Natchez. That is how I got this paper from the secretary of the Interior you hear so much about. Father Wilbur is supposed to have one, too, but he tells me he does not. I came to take you back to our old home, but Agent Wilbur will not let you go because he does not have a paper from Washington.

"I will read this to you, just as it is written."

Afterward, she explained it to them as she had to Indians at Lovelock, and patiently answered their questions.

One by one, they came to Sarah to lay their hands on her head and beg forgiveness. At last, Leggins came, his head bowed with shame. "Forgive me," he said simply. "I did not know."

"I cannot blame you for having dark hearts toward me," Sarah told them all. "But never doubt me again. I will be your friend and speak for you until the day I die."

With new hope, after hearing the words on this paper, Paiutes began to talk about seeing their old home once more. Finally, Leggins came forward and raised his hand for silence.

"Now you have heard what Thocmetony has told

us, so we must begin to get ready. All of you who want to, can go back with me and all who want to stay, can stay. If you wish to go with me, back to our sweet country and our home, step over here by my side."

Indians moved to Leggins' side—all but one. Oytes remained where he was, his head lowered, and crying.

Chief Leggins walked over to the once proud and boastful man and asked, "Why do you hang your head? You were the first one on your horse when the Bannocks came. You are the one who got us all into trouble, and but for you we would have been left in our own country! You are the cause of all our suffering, so why do you cry? I felt like crying when you got up and said, 'Come, my men! Take up your arms! We will help the Bannocks!' "

Oytes lifted his tearful eyes to Sarah, "Please," he begged, "pity me."

"I have no bad feelings for you, my brother," Sarah told him gently. "Each one of us made his own decision about what to do in the War, and we should not try to blame someone else if he made a mistake." She held out the order. "This paper says that all who want to go, can go. And I say to you, Oytes, as far as I am concerned, you are free to come with us."

"What Thocmetony says is right," Leggins admitted. "I should not have spoken to you as I did. We have all made mistakes. But now, let us go back and be happy once more in our native land."

Sarah quieted cheering Paiutes by saying, "First, we must talk with Father Wilbur."

"We will go this very night," Leggins declared.

Sarah went with them to the agency office, but it was locked and windows were dark. There was no answer to their shouts and knocks and at last, they decided to wait until the next day.

Very early in the morning Sarah walked into Agent Wilbur's office and asked him again for permission to take her people back to Nevada, but the agent refused.

"Why don't you leave?" he asked her. "You are stirring up trouble here and making the Indians restless."

"But Secretary Schurz told me you would release them! I came to take them home!"

"Get off the reservation!" he snapped. "I will not put up with the trouble you are causing. I will not let them go with you—and that is final!"

Sarah had no plans now for what to do next. Unnerved by her failure to release her people from the Yakima Reservation and more disillusioned than ever by the duplicity of white men, especially those in authority, she floundered in a sea of indecision. After talking with her brother, she decided to turn once again to the military for help. They were the only ones she could rely upon to speak the truth.

That evening, Lee went with Sarah to talk with the Indians. She told them if she stayed at the Reservation, there would only be more trouble for them. She would go to The Dalles, contact General Howard and begin again to interest the public in the plight of the Paiutes.

"I will work for you as long as I have life," she told them. "Do not ever think I have forgotten you, for I will never do that."

Sarah told her brother goodbye the next morning and started on horseback for The Dalles. Once she was settled in a small room, she wrote to General Howard, telling him the outcome of her mission.

His immediate reply asked her to come to Vancouver Barracks to serve as interpreter and teacher to the Indians there who were being cared for by soldiers. These Indians were scattered remnants of Bannock tribes who were left wandering and homeless at the close of the Bannock War.

»17

Sarah was overjoyed to be back with her good soldier friends again and with new hope kept writing to the Indian Bureau in Washington for release of Chief Leggins, Lee and the other Paiutes held at Yakima Reservation.

In the meantime she got to work teaching young Indian children at Vancouver Barracks how to read and write English. It restored her self-confidence to see their rapid progress.

Since all supplies for these Indians came from the military, Sarah showed women how to make wearing apparel for themselves and their children from army uniforms. She worked with them in making their tents more comfortable and healthful, and also taught men better working habits so they might do more to help their 'guardian angels', the soldiers, to improve the post.

Although Sarah threw herself into this work with great energy and enthusiasm, she never forgot for one minute the goal uppermost in her life. She received the greatest encouragement in her efforts from both General

and Mrs. Howard, who were sympathetic and ur
standing in their concern for the Paiutes.

The general wrote recommendation after recommendation to the Department of the Interior to redress
the wrongs done to these peaceable Indians, but to no
avail. In fact, his letters probably added to the resentment felt by the Interior Department toward the army
for what they considered to be interference in their
affairs.

Sarah spent all of her free time writing to anyone
who might be able to help. She sent many letters to
Secretary Schurz, begging him to fulfill the promises
he had made her in Washington. Her pleas were completely ignored. She wrote to others of the military who
had commanded in the west at the time Paiutes were
sent from their homeland without reason, asking them
to intercede with the government on behalf of Indians.
Many of them did so, advising the return of these Paiutes
as a matter of good faith and mercy and of justice on
the part of the United States government. For the next
two years, the plight of the Paiutes became an even
bigger issue than it had been before between the
Department of the Interior and the military.

"Send them under escort to Nevada! Send them to
Winnemucca!" General Irvin McDowell urgently wrote
in a formal army report. He requested authority to take
the responsibility of bringing the Indians back, but was
refused. Officials of the Interior Department were
offended and angered by this intrusion on their field of
endeavor, and fought back to keep the army from taking
over Indian affairs.

It may have been because of this conflict, that in
1881, when Sarah was accomplishing so much for the
good of Indians at Vancouver Barracks, with General
Howard very pleased with her handling of the school,
an order came from Washington stating these Indians
were to be taken to Fort Hall.

Once again, Sarah was appalled and confused at
this official indifference to whatever might be best for

[161

Indians. Together with General Howard, she wrote letters, begging that the Indians be allowed to stay and continue with their education, but government plans for their removal were not altered.

"Why do they do this?" Sarah cried in despair. "Indians are not animals, to be moved here and there at an owner's whim!"

Regardless of how Sarah or anyone else in sympathy with red men felt, the tribes at Vancouver were removed to Fort Hall. This put Sarah out of a job, but she had recently received five hundred dollars for her services during the Bannock War, and she wanted to go east again—this time to lecture directly to the people.

Before Sarah left, General Howard called her to his office one day with the exciting news that President and Mrs. Hayes would be visiting the fort within a few days. "I'll arrange it so you can talk with him," he said. "Perhaps you'll get a chance to remind him of those broken promises which were made when you were in Washington."

The president and his wife were very gracious, calling Sarah by name and recalling their short visit in Washington. This time, Sarah had the opportunity to speak to the president about the Paiutes as she would have done when he invited her to the capital city, had he but given her the time.

"You are a husband and a father," she told him. "Wouldn't it make you suffer to be separated from your home and family?"

Mrs. Hayes was deeply touched by Sarah's story, and tears ran down her face as she listened. The president was solemn and attentive, and when Sarah finished, he said, "I will see about it."

As days and weeks passed, and there was no visible evidence the president had "seen about it" as he had said, Sarah swallowed yet another disappointment. She couldn't help but wonder why a leader of such a great nation could be so full of politics and so empty in the heart.

As Sarah's thoughts went back to her Washington trip and its utter futility, she suddenly remembered the charming woman from Boston in the White House who had confessed her love for promoting a cause.

"She told me to write to her if I ever needed help," Sarah reflected. This had to be the time. She riffled through her belongings and found the engraved card the woman had given her. She wrote to Elizabeth Palmer Peabody that very night about her desire to go to the East to lecture.

The next day, Sarah told General Howard what she planned to do and he heartily approved. He, and others of the military, wrote recommendations of Sarah's ability and character and gave the letters to her for references. These same army officers notified influential citizens on the East Coast that Sarah Winnemucca would soon be there. The Indian princess didn't forget to write to her newspaper friend, Mr. Parker, either, and he saw to it that she got publicity.

Before she left, Sarah gave General Howard a list of her probable itinerary. "I will go to Nevada first to see my father, and then on to visit with my sister who lives near Bozeman, Montana. Please send any further letters I may get, there.

Sarah spent a day with her father and was shocked that he looked so old and frail. In her mind, her father would always be strong and upright, every inch the Big Chief of the Paiutes. When she left, she held him very close, urging him to take care of himself. The old chief murmured over and over, "My child, my child." Of course, Sarah had no way of knowing then that those were the last words she would ever hear her father speak.

Sarah stayed with her sister for a time, visiting and waiting for her mail to catch up with her. A letter came from Miss Peabody urging her to come on and assuring her of a royal welcome. This letter, combined with the days of resting and being with her dear sister, lifted Sarah's spirits and led her to feel that perhaps there was still hope. And then, something else happened, something completely unexpected, which added to Sarah's happiness.

On the same day the letter came from Miss Peabody, there was a light rapping at the door, and Elma came back from answering it to say, "There is a man to see you, sister—a white man. I do not know him."

Sarah went to the door, wondering who on earth it could be, and looked with an expression of uncertainty at the tall, lean, friendly man standing there. Then, he smiled and Sarah recognized the kindness and sincerity of someone she knew, yet she remembered it as being in a younger face.

"I can still mix up a real good fruit drink, princess."

"Lieutenant Hopkins!" she cried, grasping his hand in delight. "The last person on earth I expected to see!"

Overjoyed, Sarah brought him inside, introduced him to Elma and then sat down with him to get caught up on everything that had happened in the years they had gone separate ways.

"I started for Nevada several weeks ago," Hopkins explained. "It seems I can breathe easier out where the sagebrush grows. On the way, I heard you were here and so I took a detour." He looked at her, the old admiration still in his eyes. "You're as pretty as ever, princess. I'd have known you anywhere."

"You are very kind to say that—as you were always kind—but the years have been hard and I know I have changed," Sarah replied. "We have both changed, but we still have our happy memories of the old days at McDermit—" She broke off then, thinking of her ill-fated marriage with Lieutenant Bartlett, and her face grew sad and pensive.

Hopkins took her hands in his. "Princess, it's true, I do feel better when I'm in the West, but the real reason I came back was to find you. You must've known how I felt at McDermit, and why I asked to be transferred. I haven't changed in my feelings for you, Sarah; I can't forget you, no matter how hard I work or how far I travel."

For a moment, life took on the vagueness of a dream as Sarah looked back into the earnest brown eyes, and then, she realized he was speaking the truth. Deep down, she supposed she had been aware that he had cared for her, but there had always been the vibrant, exciting presence of Bartlett nearby to dim any thoughts she might have had about anyone else.

"Sarah," he rushed on, "I came here to ask you to marry me. I lost you once because I hesitated to tell you how I felt. Please, Sarah, we are both older and wiser and I need you—and I think you need me."

Sarah dropped her eyes in charming, almost blushing confusion. It had been so long since she had given any thought at all to her own personal wants and needs. Her life had been totally consumed with efforts to help the Paiutes, especially since the failure of her marriage.

"I do not know," she replied hesitantly. "I am not sure of my feelings for you, and you must know I am still completely involved in the fight to save my own people."

"I know, princess. You wouldn't be the 'you' I care for so deeply if you had stopped trying to help Indians. But I can help you, don't you see? With a man by your side, white people would not be so quick to slight you or treat you discourteously. I'll stay with you and work for the Paiutes. I consider it a privilege," he declared.

Lieutenant Hopkins left that day with Sarah's promise to think it over. It was such a completely new thought to her and had happened so suddenly she was confused and bewildered.

For the next few days, the constant attention on the part of Lieutenant Hopkins made Sarah realize she had overlooked many desirable qualities about the man at McDermit because, she supposed, he had been in the shadow of Bartlett's overpowering personality. But, the old kindness, sincerity and homespun warmth were still there.

"Oh, Sarah, he is such a fine man," Elma told her.

You are nearly forty years old and alone. All of us in your family would feel so much better, my sister, if you had his strong arms to support you when things are bad. Do you love him, Sarah?"

"Yes, I think I do," Sarah admitted. "Maybe not in the crazy, wild way I loved Bartlett, but in another way—maybe a better way. I know I can depend on him."

Sarah and Lieutenant Hopkins were married in January, 1882, at Helena, Montana, on their way to Boston. They had a few brief, sweet days together before Sarah was to plunge into the most intensive campaign yet on behalf of the Paiutes. She was about to meet again one of the most personable, electrifying personalities of that day, Elizabeth Palmer Peabody.

This capable woman, admired and loved throughout the land by young and old, rich and poor alike, had opened a private school of her own at the age of sixteen, and later established the first kindergarten in America for English-speaking children. She had spent the better part of her nearly eighty years trying to improve the quality of education in this country, and lecturing to young people on its values. She had written many articles on the subject, and had helped in promoting many worthy causes which had been brought to her attention. If Sarah had looked the world over, she would never have found a more genuine supporter for her work and the lecture series she had planned.

As soon as Sarah and Hopkins arrived in Massachusetts, they got in touch with Elizabeth Peabody, and the two women liked and admired each other from the first. Sarah told her in detail of her frustrating fight to help her people and of the many injustices that had been prepetrated upon them. When she had finished, her cause had become Miss Peabody's quarrel, too.

Laying aside all other projects, even her pet one of Woman Suffrage, Elizabeth Peabody immediately set about hiring halls and promoting engagements for Princess Sarah Winnemucca to lecture. She went right along with her, introducing her at each appointed place,

Elizabeth Peabody

"... I shall take it for granted that the history of Sarah's brave championship of her people's rights to living-room in their native land, to which they welcomed the whites in 1848, without price, — holding it to be God's land, as Sarah phrases it, — is known to all, it being generally understood that for a year or more she went on triumphantly, making enthusiastic friends of all who became personally acquainted with her."

and sitting in full view of audiences, on the platform while Sarah, attractive and appealing in her native Paiute costume, did the talking. It was a great relief, also, to have Hopkins along to take care of traveling details and other such problems for which neither of the ladies quite had the time.

That first year, Sarah spoke to audiences in Boston and vicinity; Providence, Rhode Island; Hartford, Connecticut; and in Pittsfield, Massachusetts where they were the invited guests of United States Senator, Henry L. Dawes. There were engagements in New York City, Newburgh, Germantown and Poughkeepsie, where she addressed students of Vassar College. The lecture tour carried her to Philadelphia, and then on to Baltimore where Sarah spoke sixty-six times, by invitation.

In her lectures, Sarah spoke of the dishonesty, cruelty and mercenary motives of Indian Agents both in the Bureau and on reservations. She told specific incidents and named names.

"The only thoroughly good agent ever sent to the Paiutes was Samuel Parrish," she declared, "and he would have been our savior had he been allowed to stay. But Mr. Parrish was replaced because he was an honest man."

She emphasized her people's loyalty to the United States government and then told how, as a reward for it, they were sent by the Department of the Interior and the president, against their will, to a strange country where they still remained, in exile, because the promise given her for their return had yet to be fulfilled.

She appealed to the average, ordinary citizens of the East, those with no official capacities, for her people's rights to a place to live in their native land, and advocated they no longer be kept as helpless wards of the government, at the mercy of whatever was politically expedient.

"If Indians are to be under supervision, let the army do it," she suggested. "Soldiers do not cheat the red men. What they speak to them is truth."

The Indian princess added a great deal of interest to her lectures by telling of the sacred social and religious customs of her people. She also told of the deep love Paiute parents have for their children, and of the respect and tender relationship between Indian brothers and sisters, husbands and wives.

One evening while lecturing in New York, Sarah described a Paiute custom called the 'Festival of Flowers.' The audience received it so favorably and it was given so much publicity, she repeated it many times afterward, by request.

"Many years ago when my people were happier than they are now," she began, "they used to celebrate the 'Festival of Flowers' in the spring. Since almost all Paiute girls are named for flowers, this occasion involved them more than the others, and was an exciting time.

"Oh, with what eagerness we girls would watch every spring for the time when we could meet with our hearts' delight, the young men whom you call *beaux*. We would all go together, each day, to see if the flowers we were named for were yet in bloom. We talked about them in our wigwams, as though we were the flowers, saying, "Oh, I saw myself today, in full bloom!" This talk delighted our families, and we had happy thoughts of the happy day when we would meet with those who admired us and who would help us sing the flower-songs which we made up as we went along. We were sorry for the girls who did not have flower names, for we knew they could not join in the flower-songs as we could.

"At last, one evening, we would hear a voice which sounded beautiful for us because we had waited so long to hear it. It was the chief, and everyone hushed to hear the words he said.

" 'My dear daughters, we are told that you have seen yourselves in the hills and in the valleys, in full bloom,' he would say. 'Five days from now, your festival day will come. I know every young man's heart stops beating while I am talking. I know how it was with me many years ago. I used to wish the 'Flower Festival' would come every day. Dear young men and young women, you are saying, "Why put it off five days?" But you all know that is our rule. It gives you time to think, and to show your sweetheart your flower.'

"All of the girls who had flower names danced along together, and those who did not stayed together. The fathers and mothers and grandfathers and grandmothers had prepared a place where we could dance. Each one gathered the flowers she was named for, and wove them into wreaths and crowns and scarves, and dressed ourselves in them.

"The girls who were named for rocks, were called rock-girls, and they found some pretty rocks which they carried, each one the rock for which she was named. If she could not find any, she carried a branch of sagebrush or a bunch of rye-grass.

"They all went marching along, each girl, in turn, singing of herself, but not as a girl. She is now a flower singing. And her sweetheart danced along by her side, helping her sing the song.

"I will tell you what we sang of ourselves, as the flowers for which we were named. 'I, Sarah Winnemucca, am a shellflower, such as I wear on my dress. My name is *Thocmetony*. I am so beautiful! Oh, come and be happy with me! I shall be beautiful while the earth lasts. Somebody will always admire me. Who will come and be happy with me in the Spirit-land? I shall be beautiful forever there. Yes, I shall be more beautiful than my shellflower, my Thocmetony! Then come, oh, come, and dance and be happy with me!'

"Our parents were waiting to welcome us home. And then, we praised the sagebrush and the rye-grass and the pretty rocks that some were named for, after which, we presented our beautiful flowers to them because they could carry none. And so, all were happy, and that closed the beautiful day."

In her lectures, Sarah never asked for money for the

'cause', but there were contributions, nonetheless. The money was put in a bank under the account name of "Paiute Education Fund," as suggested by Miss Peabody.

» 18

By the end of that year, every person in America who had a conscience pitied the Paiutes. At last, the truth had been told!

"And it took a woman to do it!" gleefully chorused those of the 'weaker sex' who had been working day and night to gain the vote for women.

"RIGHT THE WRONGS DONE TO INDIANS!" became a slogan which echoed throughout the country. Never had there been so much compassion for red men, nor so much universal feeling for a cause. Never had there been so much public eagerness to remedy this outrage and never had officials of the Indian Bureau been so alarmed.

It would be easy to imagine the scene which probably took place in the office of Henry Teller, secretary of Interior under the Arthur administration. The secretary nervously made notes in a little black memorandum book left on his desk by Mr. Schurz, while other officials of the Department squirmed uneasily in comfortable brown leather chairs.

"Why'd you let this thing get so far out of hand?" they growled.

"And just what would you have done?" Teller snapped.

"Stopped it before it got such a start! That's what!"

But, they must have realized this was no time to quarrel among themselves. They had too good a thing going to let it slip through a hole in their pockets because of one troublesome Indian woman. There had to be a way for them to stop her, and a way to destroy the sympathetic feeling for Indians she was stirring up among voters. They could not figure out exactly what to do, but it was very clear to them what they could *not* do. It was useless to deny the things Sarah Winnemucca had said, because she had told the truth, and could prove a large part of it.

At last, however, they thought of a plan. They would use a weapon often employed by weak, unprincipled persons to destroy someone who could not be dealt with otherwise. They attacked Sarah's character. Through their house organ, *Council Fire,* they made a number of accusations against the Paiute princess, and sent marked copies of the publication all over the United States.

In a clever, underhanded way, they accused Sarah of misusing money donated to Indians through her lectures, of traitorous attacks on the government, of immoral behavior and prostitution. Further, they informed the public that Sarah's own people, the Paiutes, had lost all confidence in her, and they labeled her the army's "Painted Lady."

Sarah was completely crushed by this new cruelty dreamed up by government officials to hurt her. She thought she had already dropped to the depths of despair as a result of their treatment, but this was a greater blow.

"Even this shows how little they know about us," she said to her husband. "A Paiute would not paint, even to take the path to war."

Lieutenant L. H. Hopkins, husband of Sarah Winnemucca

Hopkins was thoroughly incensed by the verbal attack on his wife, and was ready to confront the persons responsible to force a retraction from them, but Miss Peabody talked him out of it.

"It's not even worth noticing," she told him. "I'm not surprised one bit they resorted to these tactics. Any worthy cause I've ever known about had to face vicious opposition who fought with every dirty weapon they could find." To Sarah, she said, "It's no time to give up now, my dear. Speaking for myself, I'm just beginning to get up steam!"

But Sarah couldn't ignore it. She was hurt, and deeply. The cut struck clear through the core of her heart when she thought of her years of faithful service to the government, and of the many times she'd helped to promote the cause of peace in her country. This all seemed to be forgotten now.

On the night the news of this attack on Sarah's reputation hit the newsstands, she was scheduled to speak before a group of women. To accommodate the large crowd expected, the lecture was to be held in a building called, ironically enough, Soldiers' Hall. The Indian princess was so bowed-down she didn't know whether she could say a word, but gathered her strength and stepped to the podium. This time she did not speak of the Paiutes' predicament exclusively, but dealt with it as it applied to herself.

"Dear Friends, after my people were driven away from reservations by starvation, and after having every promise broken and all kinds of falsehoods told about them by agents, there was no one to take their part but a woman. Everyone knows what a woman who undertakes to act against bad men must suffer.

"My reputation has been assailed, and it is done so cunningly that I cannot prove it to be unjust. I can only protest that it *is* unjust, and say that wherever I have been known, I have been believed and trusted.

"Those who have maligned me have not known me. It is true that my people sometimes distrust me, but that is because words have been put into my mouth which have turned out to be nothing but idle wind. Promises have been made to me in high places that have not been kept, and I have had to suffer for this in the loss of some of my people's confidence.

"I have not spoken ill of others behind their backs and said fair words to their faces. I have been sincere with my own people when they have done wrong, as well as with my white brothers.

"Alas! How truly our women prophesied when they told my dear old grandfather that his white brothers, whom he loved so much, had brought sorrow to his people. Their hearts told them the truth.

"My people are ignorant of wordly knowledge, but they know what love means and what truth means. They have seen their dear ones perish around them because their white brothers have given them neither love nor truth.

"My heritage is from a people who know nothing about the history of the world, but they can see the Spirit-Father in everything. The beautiful earth talks to them of their Spirit-Father. They are innocent and simple, and they are brave and patient, and they know that black is not white. Thank you."

She turned away, but her audience would not let her go. They began to applaud and when they got to their feet, giving her a standing ovation, it was like a balm to Sarah's bruised heart.

The unanimity of opinion concerning this trumped-up charge seemed to be—"What of it?"

"What if she had used some of the donated money for herself? She had done more for the Paiutes than anyone else, hadn't she?"

"What if she had, through her lectures, maliciously attacked government officials of the Indian Bureau? She'd told the truth about them, hadn't she?"

"What if she had stayed close to the soldiers? Who wouldn't have under the same circumstances? And what if she had divorced one of them? Wasn't she a respectably married woman now?"

These people liked her and believed in her and wanted to work for her cause. They were concerned with the welfare of Indians, not with accusations made on the character of Sarah Winnemucca.

» 19

The year of 1882 brought a few hard-won victories to Sarah in the East, but news from the Far West brought sorrow and many tears. During the summer months, forty-three lodges of Paiutes had slipped away from Yakima Reservation, trying as best they could to find their way home to Nevada. They had been stopped by Agent Wilbur and his constituents who had taken them back to suffer even more because they had dared to seek their freedom.

She learned, too, that Malheur, which had been promised to Paiutes as a place to live, was no longer a reservation. It had been declared to be non-existent, by the Indian Bureau, and this land had been opened up for white settlers.

However, the worst blow was yet to fall. In the autumn General Howard wrote, informing Sarah of the death of her beloved father, Winnemucca II, Big Chief of the Paiute Nation. Although this news was very difficult for her to accept, she was glad her father was beyond reach of the white man now and could rest and be happy in the spirit-land. Her emotions were for herself, for the loneliness she felt when she realized he would not be there to meet her when she returned to Nevada, his dear face beaming with love and pride for his daughter. She tried not to think of it by keeping busy with her plans.

As another year began, conscientious citizens went ahead with their work for the red men and various new groups were organized for this specific purpose. But Sarah now had another worry added to her grief from the loss of her father. Although Hopkins continued to travel with them and take care of tiresome and troublesome details, his health was failing and he often complained of pains in his chest. The Indian princess did her best to reduce his share of the work and strain, but he seemed determined to be with her at any time when he might be needed.

As a result of Sarah's efforts, United States Senator Henry L. Dawes who had been their host in Pittsfield, authored a congressional bill which became the Dawes Act of 1887, and paved the way for American Indians to become citizens.

Elizabeth Peabody threw fresh vigor into her work, looking for new outlets for the cause, and Sarah worked with her constantly, thankful and appreciative for the friendship of such a fine and dedicated woman. Miss Peabody was extremely interested in the education of Indian children, and encouraged Sarah to think about opening a school for this purpose.

"It is one of the ways I have always dreamed of helping my people," she said simply, "for without an education they cannot adjust, or even communicate."

Sarah was fortunate to have as another friend, Miss Peabody's sister Mary, who was Mrs. Horace Mann. It was Mary Mann who suggested to Sarah she tell the story of the Paiutes in book form, and offered all assistance she could in the actual writing of the book. *Life Among the Piutes: Their Wrongs and Claims* by Sarah Winnemucca Hopkins, under the supervision of

Mary Mann
(Mrs. Horace Mann)

Mary Mann's Preface to Sarah's book.
"My editing has consisted in copying the original manuscript in correct orthography and punctuation, with occasional emendations by the author, of a book which is an heroic act on the part of the writer . . . . It is the first outbreak of the American Indian in human literature, and has a single aim — to tell the truth as it lies in the heart and mind of a true patriot, and one whose knowledge of the two races gives her an opportunity of comparing them justly."

Mrs. Horace Mann, was published in 1883.

In that same year, encouraged by her many friends, Sarah petitioned Congress to reactivate Malheur Reservation for her people, to restore their rights, and to return the Paiutes from Yakima Reservation to their homeland.

A Massachusetts representative presented the petition for her, which read:

> WHEREAS, the tribe of Paiute Indians that formerly occupied the greater part of Nevada, and now diminished by its sufferings and wrongs to one-third of its original number, has always kept its promise of peace and friendliness to the whites since they first entered their country, and has of late been deprived of the Malheur Reservation decreed to them by President Grant.
>
> I, SARAH WINNEMUCCA HOPKINS, a grand-daughter of Captain Truckee, who promised friendship for his tribe to General Fremont, whom he guided into California, and served through the Mexican War, together with the undersigned friends who sympathize in the cause of my people, so petition the Honorable Congress of the United States to restore to them said Malheur Reservation, which is well watered and timbered, and large enough to afford homes and support for them all, where they can enjoy lands in severalty without losing their tribal relations, so essential to their happiness and good character, and where their citizenship, implied in this distribution of land, will defend them from the encroachments of the white settlers, so detrimental to their interests and their virtues. And especially do we petition for the return of that portion of the tribe arbitrarily removed from Malheur Reservation after the Bannock War to the Yakima Reservation on the Columbia River, in which removal families were ruthlessly separated, and have never ceased to pine for husbands, wives, and children, which restoration was pledged to them by the Secretary of the Interior in 1880, but has not been fulfilled."

Thousands of supporters for the cause signed this paper. After it was presented to Congress, it was referred to certain committees, where it was tossed about from one to the other for a time.

But even as this petition was making the rounds, one of the things for which Sarah had worked for so long came to pass. The Paiutes who had been held at Yakima Reservation were allowed to return home to Nevada. No transportation was provided and they had to make it back any way they could, but most of them managed. Some settled around McDermit and others scattered out through the sageland wherever they could find food.

There were some notes of sadness in the return home. Leggins never got to see his "sweet" country again, because by this time he had become blind. And Oytes, warped in mind and body by the years of starvation and inhuman treatment, and hounded by guilt, again turned hostile. With a renegade band, he traveled over the country, wreaking vengence on any white man he could find.

Sarah spent a great deal of time interviewing committees responsible for recommendations in her petition, but she was not successful in regaining Malheur Reservation for Paiutes. Instead, Congress passed a bill in July of 1884, granting lands in severalty to her people who had come back from Yakima and to her father's band, on Pyramid Reservation. Immediate enforcement of the bill was entrusted to Mr. Teller.

This bit of legislation was also intended to abolish the Agency at Pyramid, and this was the understanding of military officials who sent soldiers from army headquarters of the Pacific to drive off usurping white settlers. After this had been done, General Pope dispatched a message to the Department of the Interior to the effect that settlers had left Pyramid Reservation without resistance.

Commissioner Price of the Indian Bureau then wrote to Sarah he was ready to cooperate with her in establishing a school for Indian children. He promised her the position of teacher, with a government salary, and urged her to come to Nevada as soon as possible. Sarah should have been beside herself with joy, but her long and bitter dealings with white officials had left her distrustful.

"I wonder if this is really true," she remarked to her husband.

"I believe it is. I think this time they will do what they say. I trust the commissioner," he replied positively.

Miss Peabody concurred in his opinion. "This is what we've been hoping for," she told Sarah. "It's like a dream come true." And she began planning at once, deciding where she'd put all of the helpful materials she'd devised for kindergartens.

Even Mary Mann thought it was just wonderful. She had not a doubt nor fear that the commissioner's offer was anything but the truth.

Only Sarah remained unconvinced. "I do not believe him," she persisted. "He does not write the truth."

Because of her great respect for Sarah's judgment, Mary Mann wrote Commissioner Price, herself, asking him to reaffirm his intentions regarding both the government Indian school and Sarah. The reply she received from him repeated the same message he had written to the princess. Everyone but Sarah believed she had at last won a victory from the Indian Bureau, and they tried to convince her of this.

Still, Sarah kept protesting, "In all of my lifetime, I have never known even one man in the Department of the Interior or Indian Affairs to speak the truth. Why should they start now?"

Then, one day, from army headquarters of the Pacific, a letter came from Adjutant General Kelton notifying Sarah officially that soldiers had cleared all white settlers off Pyramid Reservation. He added a little personal note, advising her to come back immediately and told her how happy the military men were that she could be the one to lead her people onto lands which would be their own, thus starting a new and better life for them.

This message broke Sarah's resistance to the idea of returning to Nevada now. The military had always been on her side, and General Kelton had proved his friendship with the Paiutes many times during his twenty years of service in the Far West. She decided right then to head for home.

She left her work in the East in capable hands. Elizabeth Peabody promised to keep the cause alive and rolling and Mary Mann agreed to promote the sale of Sarah's book. Money earned from it was to be deposited in the bank along with contributions.

With hope in her heart, Sarah once again turned toward the West.

» 20

It was late in August of 1884 when Sarah and her husband stepped from the train at Wadsworth, Nevada, just as the first clear blue light of early morn broke upon the sageland. A cool, gentle breeze of high desert country brushed across Sarah's cheeks, as if to welcome her home. Everything seemed just the same as when she had left it, and she found it was, even to the same old trouble with the Indian Bureau!

Not a day had passed before she learned the promises made by Commissioner Price were untruths, just as she had predicted. White settlers had moved back on lands supposedly set aside for Indians as soon as soldiers left, and the agency had not been abolished.

Secretary of the Interior Teller had completely ignored the Congressional document granting lands to Paiutes and the new, politically appointed agent at Pyramid Reservation was a carbon copy of others with whom Sarah had dealt through the long years.

Wearily, she made the rounds again, engaging in useless talks with indifferent or downright-rude officials, and obtaining nothing at all for her people.

turn, she buried her head in the curve
shoulder and sobbed, "What will they

held his wife close, he felt shame and
e. He felt an agonizing helplessness
not stop them from cruelly hurting
the woman he loved and the race of people to which
she belonged.

"How much more is my princess supposed to
endure?" he whispered.

Sarah found her mind a welter of confusion. Sup-
pressed by this latest deception and physically ill for the
first time in her life, she was on the verge of giving up.

Yet, even though she was low in both spirit and in
strength, Sarah had inherited a quality which is char-
acteristic of Indian chiefs—a sense of duty to their people.
That is why, no doubt, she decided to return to the
source of her strength, the Paiutes, and make her plans
after staying with them for awhile.

That fall and winter, Sarah and her husband lived
among the Indians and she was reunited with her
brothers. Although she missed the strong presence of
her father, after a time Sarah began to find peace of
mind within the family circle of the campfire. In the
mystic gleams of flickering flames, the Indian princess
once again began to dream her dreams, and, surrounded
by people who loved her and believed in her, she dared
to hope they might come true.

"If I could start a school of my own for Paiute
children," Sarah said, putting a dream into words. "I
could teach them to talk and read English, and to write.
I could teach them the history of America and how to
figure with numbers."

"I have a little money," Hopkins spoke up. "We'll
buy some land so you can start your school."

"I do not know," her brother Natchez told him
doubtfully, "White men do not want Indians to have
anything, and they would know you were buying the
land for my sister. It would take big pay."

"I can at least try," Hopkins insisted. "And—we could work the land."

"Yes, and in the school, I could teach them how to help themselves," Sarah kept on. "Indian children learn fast."

The princess wrote to Elizabeth Peabody, telling her everything that had happened. "I can gain nothing from the Indian Bureau, and my military friends have done all they can. Any progress now will be only what I can do myself."

She also disclosed to her eastern friend, plans of starting a school of her own if her husband could buy some land. She inquired about the amount in the education fund and royalties from the book.

Sarah received a reply by return mail. It was full of enthusiasm and encouraging news. The education fund carried a balance of a little over five hundred dollars, and the book was selling well. "Since it is the first literary contribution of an American Indian," she wrote, "it has great appeal, and the sympathy for red men at this time makes it popular, too." She didn't know the exact amount of royalties since Mary Mann had not collected them yet, but promised to let her know very soon.

"Your plan sounds just great to me," she added. "Mary and I will help all we can, and I'll be getting materials ready to send."

As Natchez had predicted, however, when Hopkins tried to get property, he was blocked at every turn because white settlers did not want an Indian school outside of Indian land.

Sarah wrote Elizabeth Peabody about this latest disappointment and described the school which was currently being held for children on the reservation. "A teacher, chosen by the agent, has taught children to sing a few hymns. Of course, they do not understand the words, but can repeat, and this makes a show in case an official comes to inspect." She closed with, "It is not to the advantage of government officials to

[187

educate Indians."

Soon afterward, in the spring of 1885, as soon as the administration changed, Elizabeth Peabody packed her bags and made a trip to Washington to tell "young Grover Cleveland" about the Paiutes.

That same spring, much to the surprise of everyone and to the delight of Sarah, her family and her friends, Leland Stanford, the newly-elected United States senator from California, deeded one hundred and sixty acres of land near Lovelock Nevada, to Natchez Winnemucca. Nobody ever knew why, for sure, although there was much speculation. Hopkins said possibly Miss Peabody had talked him into it, but Sarah thought it might have been another move on his part to ease his conscience about the Indian lands his Central Pacific Railroad had taken.

Sarah did not puzzle long about *why* he did it. The only thing which mattered now was that they had the land they needed, and could actually get started on plans for a school to help Indian children.

She notified Elizabeth Peabody at once, and with great joy, that woman started the ball rolling in earnest. From further contributions and royalties on Sarah's book, she was able to send seven hundred dollars in cash to pay for surveying, fencing and buying seed for planting. In addition to the money she sent canvas for tents, a wagon, horses, harness, agricultural tools and food to last them until something could be grown on their land. Later, when the school actually opened, she sent pencils, paper, a blackboard, chalk and books.

Sarah started teaching the young Indians early in the summer. She had planned to use a tent for a schoolhouse, but the twenty-four Paiute children living within two miles of Lovelock who came early every morning to stay all day would have stretched the tent to more than capacity so their classes were held outside, in a brush arbor.

She began by teaching her students the military drill with which she had become so familiar during her years at Fort McDermit. Her purpose being to discipline their bodies and minds to rhythmical motion. She also taught them to sing "The Star Spangled Banner" and a few hymns by interpreting words into the Paiute language so they would understand the meaning. This led quite naturally into lessons teaching them to speak English, and then came reading and the writing of it. Soon, she began teaching them to draw, and to work with numbers.

Sarah gave her students initiative in conversation by asking them to say something in the Paiute language and then teaching them to say the same thing in English. Words were written on the board for them to copy and then find in books. These happy, round-faced youngsters never forgot a word once they learned it; in fact, they were so entranced with their new vocabulary and the writing of it, they scrawled words all over wooden fences in Lovelock.

At frequent intervals, Sarah wrote to Miss Peabody reporting on the progress which was being made. She was proud of her pupils' accomplishments, and usually enclosed samples of their work. Her eastern friend was amazed and overjoyed, not only because of the ability of these Indian children but also because of the over-tones of happiness and contentment she could read between the lines of Sarah's letters. At last, at last, something was going well for her.

Sarah's family got to work clearing and irrigating the acreage as soon as they were certain this land really belonged to Natchez. Now, classroom work alter-nated with outdoor exercise and helping on the farm. Sarah had hopes that in time the venture would become a self-supporting boarding school. Children were taught how to work the soil, plant, weed, and care for livestock. In this way she felt she could teach them a sense of personal responsibility for self-support.

The men helped Sarah supervise work on the farm, and that, together with their own chores, kept them busy every minute. The first year they had ninety acres

[189

of wheat and barley, vegetable gardens, chickens and pigs. Sarah loved her family for pitching in to help, although she was very concerned about her husband's failing health. She now knew it was only a matter of time until she would be without him, but courageously concealed her anguish by keeping busy with the students.

Before fall, Sarah realized the brush arbor, although it served her purpose quite well during warm months, could not be used as a class room all winter long. Miss Peabody was cognizant of this fact as well and wrote her to get estimates from dealers in building materials and from carpenters in the area on the cost of a schoolhouse. Friends in the East raised the needed money and by the time cold weather arrived, Indian pupils had a substantial building in which to attend classes. It also included living quarters for Sarah and her husband.

In return for money sent, the Indian princess mailed receipts, although this was not required of her, and never spent any of it on things which were not definitely specified. The memory of cruel and untrue accusations made against her by government officials was still a deep hurt and made her overly cautious.

The school became a sort of enlarged home for Indian children and Sarah taught the girls to cook and keep house. She also taught them to sew, using cloth sent through the mail by her friends. This skill attracted Indian boys as well and before long, all students were busily stitching away—girls on dresses and blouses and boys on shirts.

Sarah arranged pictures on walls of the rooms to make them attractive places for the children. There were colored drawings of cats, dogs, horses, birds, flowers and trees, all of which were sent from the east, and the children thought they had never seen anything so beautiful.

They were fascinated by huge, colorful maps which came, too, but the most bewildering thing of all, perhaps, was a big clock which came one day as a surprise. When it arrived, Sarah hung it high, near her desk, to allow the children to get used to it. Then, she taught them its proper name, in English, and how it is used. Eventually, they all learned to tell the time of day.

In her teaching of these Indian children, Sarah was very careful to include the past with the present, for she felt, and very deeply, traditions of the old ones should never be overlooked, or forgotten. Indians shared a common heritage which Sarah wanted them to remember, always.

She taught the children about nature and how to observe habits of plants and animals. Every year when cool days came again, after the desert's dry, hot time, she would take them on an excursion into nearby hills to gather pine nuts. She made them understand that to Indians this was not just a matter of gathering food, but a ceremony of great significance. She told them, too, this had always been her favorite time of year, and the thing she liked best to do.

From Sarah, children learned that before the coming of the white man, native pinon pine trees covered the high country in Paiute-land, and nuts from this tree had supplied the most nourishing food available to them. Every fall, whole tribes went into the mountains to gather pine nuts and it was one of the most sacred of their customs.

Each season, before they started, a dance was held in reverence of the pinon tree and prayers were sung for both a good harvest and for themselves, that they would feel well on the trip and not be sick.

"Since the pine nuts belong to the pinon trees, and the trees belong to the mountain, and the mountain is part of the earth," Sarah would explain to these children, "we always ask permission of the earth and the mountain and the tree to take pine nuts from them. And after the nuts are gathered, before we go home, we always say, 'thank you.' "

In the old days, the cones were knocked from trees with long poles, gathered into baskets, and put into great pits for roasting. Then, nuts were cracked between rocks to open the shells and this had to be done with care so not to mash the soft, oily kernels. Indians ate these nuts as they came from the shell or ground them into a flour which they mixed with water for soup. Any nuts which were not used immediately were stored in the ground or in mounds and covered with grasses and mud.

Sarah explained all of this carefully so the children of a younger generation would know the ways of their ancestors. She actually let them do some of the things she told about, such as roasting a few pine nuts at a time in a flat reed winnowing tray by adding clinkers from a campfire. She demonstrated the art of keeping coals flipping about in the tray so nuts would be roasted without burning the basket.

Another thing pupils learned how to do was to heat water in a liquid-tight jug made of grasses and stems of plants. Since a basket could not be set over the fire, the procedure was to throw red hot coals into the water, keeping the jug bouncing about in a smooth constant motion. By adding more and more coals at intervals, water could be brought to a boil.

All of these things added interest and variety to studies in Sarah's school, and she never had discipline problems. It was a happy experience for children to learn, but a greater joy to Sarah, who knew she was helping them. More than anything else, she wanted to educate Indian children so they could become teachers, themselves, and go on with the further educating of their race. It was her hope, too, that perhaps sometime government schools could be transformed into centers of life for Indians.

By now, there were a few government boarding schools but Sarah's school at Lovelock was the only all-Indian one and the best-known. Enrollment grew and she had on a waiting list four hundred requests from Indian parents who wanted their children placed in her school. Even though Sarah didn't have the vitality she'd had in former days and became exhausted easily, it was a source of great disappointment to her that she didn't have facilities to accommodate them.

With the hope of enabling the chieftain's daughter to erect another building and to make other necessary adjustments to take all of these children in, Elizabeth Peabody asked the government to appropriate necessary money for this worthy cause. Officials, of course, did not think it wise.

Undaunted, Elizabeth had yet another idea. What a wonderful gesture it would be on the part of Mr. Leland Stanford if he would crown his gift of land which had made Sarah's school possible in the first place, with making it a branch of learning affiliated with his own great university.

And who knows? It might have happened in just this way but time ran out for Sarah. She was completely exhausted and ill. She gave up and the heart went out of her school. As Miss Peabody expressed it, "Without the Paiute princess, the Indian school can never be the same."

Lieutenant Hopkins had died that year, in 1887. To Sarah, who relied on his strength and quiet goodness, it was though a part of her own self had ceased to be. This grief, together with the many years of privation and exposure, resentment, disappointments and mental suffering, left her without the stamina to continue.

Sarah stayed on in Lovelock for nearly two years. Then, when the warm winds came again, went with her brothers to visit Elma who still lived near Bozeman, Montana, but she did not return to Nevada with them. Instead, she stayed with her sister, and for the first time in her life, perhaps, had no plans for things to come.

Undoubtedly, her mind dwelled on past events—unnecessary sufferings of her people, lack of communication with government officials and of her untiring efforts to bring about a lasting peace between Indians and the white race. And then, in 1891, peace came at last to her. It was in the fall, in October, in the "gathering-of-the-pinenut-time."

In 1971, Nevada's first historical marker honoring a woman, Sarah Winnemucca, was erected off U.S. 95 inside the east entrance to the McDermit Indian Reservation on the site of the old officers' quarters. Engraved on the marker is: ". . . . . she was a believer in the brotherhood of mankind."

For Further Reference

This book is focused on an individual. For those who wish to pursue a study of Nevada Paiutes, the Bannock War of 1878 or of early Nevada, the following publications are suggested:

Angel, Myron. *Thompson and West History of Nevada, 1881.*

Arnold, Royal Ross. *Indian Wars of Idaho.*

Bancroft, Hubert H. *History of Nevada, 1888.*

Bancroft, Hubert H. *History of Oregon, 1888.*

Brimlow, George F. *The Bannock Indian War of 1878.*

Cook, Sherburne F. *Indians of North America — Nevada.*

Dale, Edward E. *Indians of the Southwest.*

Davis, Samuel Post. *History of Nevada.*

Dictionary of American Biography.

Dictionary of American Indians.

Fletcher, Fred Nathaniel. *Early Nevada.*

Forbes, Jack D. *Native Americans of California and Nevada.*

Forbes, Jack D. *Nevada Indians Speak.*

Ghent. *The Road to Oregon.*

Haglund, E.A. *The Washoe, Paiute and Shoshone Indians of Nevada.*

Harrington, M.R. *American Archaeology and Ethnology, V 25.*

Hodge, Frederick Webb. *Handbook of American Indians.*

— Hopkins, Sarah Winnemucca. *Life Among the Piutes—Their Wrongs and Claims.*

— Howard, Oliver Otis. *Famous Indian Chiefs I Have Known.*

Howard, Oliver Otis. *My Life & Experiences Among Our Hostile Indians.*

Kelly, Isabel. *Paiute Indians.*

Lillard, Richard Gordon. *Desert Challenge, an Interpretation of Nevada.*

Meacham, A.B. *Wigwam and Warpath.*

Morgan, Dale L. *Humboldt, Highroad of the West.*

Nevada State Museum Anthropology Papers, No. 2.

Oregon Historical Society Reports, V 51, 53, 54.

Peabody, Elizabeth Palmer. *The Paiutes—Report of Sarah Winnemucca's School.*

Shepperson, Wilbur S. *Retreat to Nevada.*

Stewart, Omer Call. *Paiute Indians: Northern Paiute.*

Stewart, Omer Call. *The Northern Paiute Bands.*

Turner, Katharine C. *Red Men Calling on the Great White Father.*

The Bureau of Ethnology Yearbooks.

Underhill, R.M. *The Northern Paiute Indians of California & Nevada.*

Wheat, Margaret M. *Survival Arts of the Primitive Paiutes.*

Who's Who in America (Historical Volume).

Wren, Thomas. *A History of Nevada.*

Information & documents may be obtained from historical and university libraries of Nevada, Oregon, Idaho and Montana.

Information & documents from National Archives through General Services Administration, Washington, D.C. contained in the National Archives Special file, "The Case of Sarah Winnemucca."

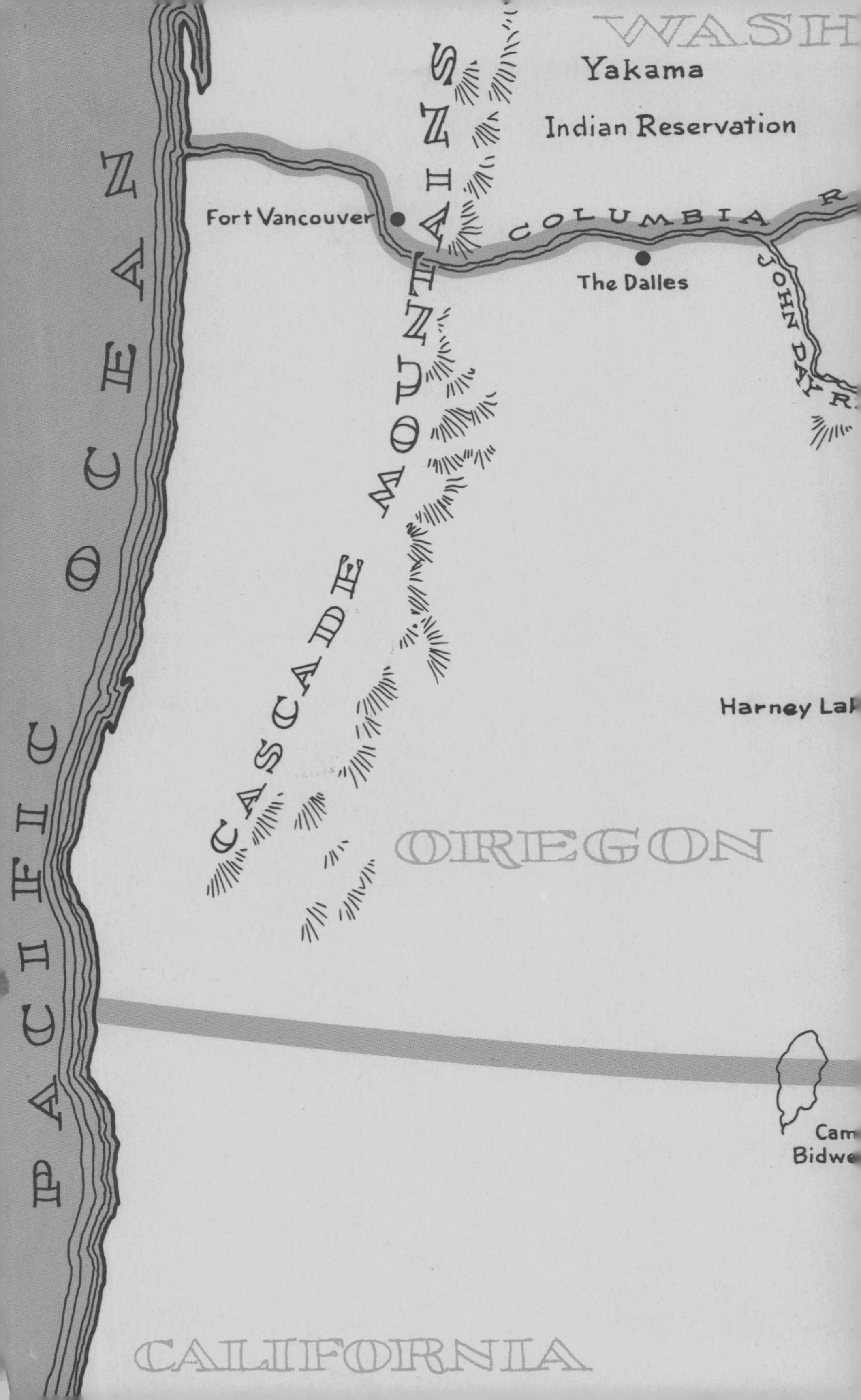

WASH
Yakama
Indian Reservation
Fort Vancouver
COLUMBIA R
The Dalles
JOHN DAY R.
CASCADE MOUNTAINS
PACIFIC OCEAN
Harney Lak
OREGON
Cam
Bidwe
CALIFORNIA